Some Press Opinions on the First Edition

Saturday Review.—" Any gentleman about to publish may create, in his mind's eye, without great difficulty, the appearance of the masterpiece he intends. There can be no more trustworthy guide ' For those that think in type and ink ' than this clearly written and admirably printed handbook."

New Review.—" A modest volume, but one which is pretty in its vermilion lettering upon clear white buckram . . . all professional writers ought to possess."

Daily Telegraph.—" Abundant information is stored within its pages ; in short, no one whose bent is literary will take up the book without learning some fact in typography which will both interest and enlighten him."

Literary World.—" With the aid of this guide, one intending to publish can go to his publisher not wholly ignorant of the technicalities of bookmaking, and others can pick up a good deal of interesting information."

Publishers' Circular.—" Writers will save themselves much trouble and unnecessary labour if they diligently master its contents, and the knowledge so gained will in turn benefit the printers."

The Bookman.—" This is a practical handbook for authors, publishers and printers, on types, proofs, stereotyping, binding, copyright, registration, and other matters relating to the issuing of books."

The Speaker.—" It is the outcome of wide and practical experience in the making of all sorts and sizes of choice and artistic books."

Birmingham Daily Post.—" Book-lovers as well as book-makers are certain to be interested in a work, modestly entitled ' Some Notes on Books and Printing, a Guide for Authors and Others,' by Mr. Charles T. Jacobi, the Examiner in Typography to the City and Guilds of London Institute, which is being issued from the Chiswick Press, of which Mr. Jacobi is manager."

SOME NOTES ON
BOOKS & PRINTING

1790—1902

SOME NOTES ON BOOKS AND PRINTING

A GUIDE FOR AUTHORS PUBLISHERS & OTHERS

By CHARLES T. JACOBI

MANAGING PARTNER OF THE
CHISWICK PRESS

NEW AND ENLARGED EDITION

LONDON: CHARLES WHITTINGHAM & CO.
AT THE CHISWICK PRESS, TOOKS COURT
CHANCERY LANE. MDCCCCII

First printed, November, 1892 (1000 *copies*).
Reprinted, March, 1902 (500 *copies*).

PREFACE TO NEW EDITION

IN issuing a fresh edition of this work, I have introduced some additional features in the type specimens given at the end of the volume.

The literary part has been revised and much enlarged, and I trust it will be found even more useful than the earlier issue of this work.

I am greatly indebted to Mr. F. Howard Collins for the chapter on the Index, and for many kind suggestions and much help in the literary portion of the work. I also thought, as illustrated books are so much in demand nowadays, that the article bearing on Methods of Illustration was worthy of a fuller treatment than that accorded to it ten years ago, when process engraving was not so developed as at the present time. I therefore persuaded Mr. Walter Boutall, Chairman of Messrs. Vaus and Crampton, Ltd., who has had a long and varied experience of mechanical processes, to enlarge the chapter previously devoted to this subject, and for this I tender him my best thanks.

I am also obliged to Mr. C. R. Rivington, the clerk of the Worshipful Company of Stationers, for looking over the proof of the chapter relating to copyright.

CHAS. T. JACOBI.

March, 1902.

PREFACE TO FIRST EDITION

THE present volume is practically a revised reprint of my little book "On the Making and Issuing of Books," which Mr. Elkin Mathews published for me in the spring of last year. The appreciation with which that volume met, and the inquiries I have had for it since the limited edition was exhausted, have encouraged me to re-issue it in a different form, with the addition of many typographical specimens, and a few samples of really good papers suitable for printing purposes.

All the types shown here are in use at the Chiswick Press, but founts which are peculiar to that office have not been included, in order that the utility of the book for general reference may not be in any way limited.

CHAS. T. JACOBI.

October, 1892.

CONTENTS

SOME NOTES ON
BOOKS AND PRINTING

CHAPTER I

THE MANUSCRIPT

THE proper preparation of the manuscript is one of the first and most important steps in the making of a book. A clearly written MS., especially if by an unknown author, will often appeal to a publisher, when he would pass over the same matter in a scarcely legible form.

In writing, it is preferable to use a medium size of paper, such as quarto—copy-book size—for two important reasons. If additions or alterations of any extent have to be made to any one page, there is less matter to re-copy than if the paper be folio or foolscap. The latter is too high at the top or commencement of each page for writing to be done without effort or strain : a consideration not to be despised when many thousand words have to be

B

penned.   A smaller paper makes an objectionable
thickness of MS. when a book is finished.

The paper used may be without lines, but it is
better for regularity, and for estimating the number
of words, if ruled paper be used, and the writing be
on the lines.   Each leaf should be separate, and
not in folded sections, to facilitate turning over.

One other suggestion is as follows: If the
author wishes to make for his own convenience a
rough draft of his manuscript, he should adopt a
paper with lines rather widely ruled, or, if he has
closely ruled paper, should write on alternate lines.
This allows of space for interpolations and emen-
dations.

The writing must of course be on one side only,
for it is necessary in bookwork that each compositor's portion or "take" should finish at the end
of a paragraph, and if the paper be written on
both sides the scissors cannot be used by the
overseer who allots the portions to each compositor.

A blank margin of one inch from the left-hand
edge should always be left: it allows room for
small alterations, and also for remarks and instructions to the printer.

Each leaf *must* be distinctly paged in con-
secutive order from the first to the last, for on the
MS. arriving in the printer's room it is all distributed in sections here and there, and unless this
has been done, great and unnecessary trouble is
caused to everyone concerned.

It is, however, advisable that all manuscript should be typewritten. In many instances publishers now make it a *sine quâ non* : they will not even "consider" any work until it is in this form.

Most frequently the MS. is simply sent to a typewriter to be copied; but now that a really good machine can be purchased for about ten pounds, it is very much better in every way for the author himself to learn it, and thus do away with the pen entirely for all work intended for the printer. A friend of the author's has used a typewriter for some years, and he asserts that it is no exaggeration to say that, with ordinary attention, at the end of the first month, after writing each day for an hour or more, the speed will more than equal that possible with the pen ; and that with further practice this speed will be increased. The result is so good that it can always be treated as a first proof—to the great saving of the author's pocket. Another great advantage with typewriting is, that by placing a piece of thin paper and the ordinary black carbon paper over the one to be typewritten, a duplicate can be obtained as good as the one which will be sent to the printers. By this means any anxiety about the MS. being lost in transmission, or by fire—as occurred in the historic case of Carlyle's "French Revolution"— is removed, and the expense saved of postal registration and the insurance which is advisable with valuable matter. And to the young author all his writing is valuable before it has been submitted to a publisher!

It may be mentioned here that though the MS. be typewritten it is paid for at the "manuscript" rate.   In London there are three distinct rates paid for type-setting : (*a*) where the copy is in print, and an absolute facsimile is to be made; (*b*) where the copy is in print, but is to be set up in a different type, measure, or width ; (*c*) where the copy is wholly or partly written or typewritten.

Avoid all interlineations : if necessary, cut the sheet in two where the addition is required, and gum in the slip containing the added matter.

On reading the copy over, should it be desired to commence a new paragraph, a bracket mark thus [should be put in front of the first word, and " new par." written in the margin against it.

Should, on the contrary, a paragraph already written as such appear unnecessary, a line should be drawn from the end of the last word of the first paragraph to the first word of the next, and a marginal note made, "run on."

Either of these alterations concerning paragraphs should *only* be made in the MS., as they are expensive when in type, for they often entail the alteration of a large amount of subsequent matter.

The following abbreviations, agreed to at the International Shorthand Congress, 1887, are a great convenience, and save writing many thousand useless letters in ordinary copy.   The best way to learn them—and they are worth learning—

is to write out several times both the shortened form and the word for which it stands.

Longhand Abbreviations recognized by Printers.

About, ab^t.
Account, acc^t.
Afternoon, aft^n.
Again, ag^n.
Against, ag^{st}.
Among, am^g.
Amount, am^t.

Because, *bec.*
Been, b^n.
Between, *btwn.*
Brought, bro^t.

Caught, c^t.
Chairman, ch^n.
Circumstance, cir^{ce}.
Committee, com^e.
Could, c^d.

Difference, dif^{ce}.
Different, dif^t.
Difficult, dif^{elt}.
Difficulty, dif^{clty}.

Evening, ev^g.
Every, ev^y.
Extraordinary, xtr^y.

For, *f.*
From, f^m.
Further, fu^r.

General, gen^l.
Government, gov^t.
Great, g^t.

Had, h^d.
Have, *h.*
However, how^r.

Importance, imp^{ce}.
Important, imp^t.

Large, *lge.*

Meeting, mt^g.
Might, m^t.
Morning, m^g.

Notwithstanding, $notw^g$.

Objection, obj^n.
O'clock, *o'c.*
Of, *o.*
Opinion, op^n.
Opportunity, opp^y.
Other, o^r.
Ought, o^t.

Particular, $part^r$.

Question, q^n.

Said, s^d.

Several, *sev^l*.
Shall, *sh*.
Should, *sh^d*.

That, *t*.
The, /.
Their, there, *th^r*.
Though, *tho*.
Through, *thro*.
Together, *tog^r*.

Very, *v^y*.

Whenever, *when^r*.
Wherever, *where^r*.
Whether, *wh^r*.
Which, *w^h*.
Whichever, *which^r*.
With, *w*.
Without, *w^t*.

Would, *w^d*.

Yesterday, *yest^y*.
You, *y*.
Your, *y^r*.

Terminations.
Ance, ence, *ce*.
Ever, *r*.
Ing, *g*.
Ion, sion, tion, *n*.
Ment, *m^t*.

Sunday, *Sun*.
Monday, *Mon*.
Tuesday, *Tues*.
Wednesday, *Wed*.
Thursday, *Thurs*.
Friday, *Fri*.
Saturday, *Sat*.

Most printing establishments of any note have their "customs of the house" as regards orthography, the use of capital letters, punctuation, etc., though they may be unwritten laws. As a rule these details can be left to the printer. If any particular style is required, a general direction should be given to the printer when handing in the copy, any little deviation being remedied in the proofs. It is the fashion now to reduce the number of capitals as far as possible, except for proper names.

Some correspondence has recently taken place in the literary press concerning these customs and styles, which differ in the leading printing offices, and it is to be hoped that greater uniformity will be the result.

The beginnings of paragraphs should always be boldly indicated by insetting the first word, say an inch further towards the right than the other lines.

The following underlinings are universally employed in MS. to indicate italic, small capitals, and capitals :

italic = *italic*

small capitals = SMALL CAPITALS

caps & small caps = CAPS AND SMALL CAPS

capitals = CAPITALS

Titles of works or periodicals are underlined or placed within inverted commas, to make them distinct; the printer using his discretion, except in the case of special instructions from the author.

Extract matter included in the text—which is generally set in a smaller type—should be clearly shown, either by marking it down the side from beginning to end with a vertical line (in coloured ink or pencil is the best plan), or by setting the whole well towards the right of the other matter.

Footnotes should each have a corresponding reference, and where possible should be written immediately after the word to which they refer. Figures, [1][2][3][4], are to be preferred for this purpose.

It is most important to remember that pages are not the same as leaves : a leaf, being printed on both sides, is equal to two pages. The one side, corresponding to the right-hand page of this book, being technically called the "recto"; and the other side, the left-hand page, back, or obverse, the " verso."

With regard to the corrections in the proofs it must be remembered that the more carefully a book is written, the less expense will be incurred for "author's corrections." This charge is often a great source of contention between the author, publisher, and printer, and is altogether unsatisfactory. A printer is bound, with certain reservations, to follow the copy supplied, and if he does that, and the author makes no alterations, there are no author's corrections and nothing to dispute. But should there be many alterations, they may prove disastrously troublesome and expensive, besides delaying the work.

The charges made for corrections are based on the time consumed in making them, and are very difficult to check, even by an expert.

A page of type may contain two, three or more thousands of letters, every word being built up letter by letter and line by line, till the page is complete. A small correction, trivial as it may seem to the inexperienced, may possibly involve much trouble to the printer, and the labour expended on it not being apparent, is only appreciated by a practical man. A word inserted or deleted may cause a page to be altered throughout line by line, and a few words may possibly affect several pages.

Therefore, if possible, in making verbal corrections always substitute words of an equal length to those removed—this is money saved in corrections.

"Extras" comprise the foregoing author's corrections, because the labour likely to be involved is not apparent when a volume is put in hand; extraneous or miscellaneous matter, such as tables, foreign languages, etc., being expensive in composition; and all charges for types smaller than the body of the work. In the case of printed copy, termed "reprint," the extras can be accurately estimated.

If it is necessary to correct a work in type, and the alterations are likely to disarrange lines and possibly pages, proofs in "galley" or "slip" form should be ordered. In America first proofs are generally in this form, and it will save an inexperienced author much expense if he *always* has them so. This means a little more trouble to the printer, but to the author or publisher less expense in the long run, because corrections can be more easily effected in slips.

In marking corrections for the printer certain recognized signs and symbols are used which express concisely what is required. We give on page 11 the principal characters used, and the corrections as marked by a skilled person; on page 10 is shown the type corrected accordingly.

These corrections are explained in detail on the verso of the marked page.

In correcting a proof always ink the wrong letter or word through, and insert the alteration *in the margin*, not in the middle of the printed matter, because it is apt to be overlooked without a marginal reference. To keep the different corrections distinct, finish each one off with a stroke thus / And to make the alterations more clear, if they are many, mark those on the left-hand portion of the page in the left margin, and those on the right-hand in the right margin.

We have already said that as corrections and alterations are occasionally a source of dispute between publisher, author, and printer, it is most important that these corrections should be clearly and concisely made. Frequently proofs are unnecessarily cut about, which makes it difficult for the compositor to follow, and hence he consumes more time in making these alterations. This waste of time applies also to the reader, whose duty it is to see that the author's corrections have been properly effected.

It is also recommended that all old proofs bearing author's corrections or alterations be retained. They are sometimes necessary for the verification of charges, or in checking some presumed "error of the press," which has been discovered at a later stage.

On receiving a proof the first thing to be done is to read it through carefully, *not noticing the sense*,

These corrections are explained in detail on the verso of the marked page. [In correcting a proof always ink the wrong letter or word through, and insert the alteration *in the margin*, not in the middle of the printed matter, because it is Apt to be overlooked without a marginal reference.

To keep the different corrections distinct, finish each one off with a stroke thus / And to make the alterations more clear, if they are many, mark those on the left-hand portion of the page in the left margin, and those on the right-hand in the right margin.

We have already said that as corrections and alterations are occasionally a source of dispute between publisher, author, and printer, it is most important that these corrections should be clearly and concisely made. Frequently *proofs* are unnecessarily cut about, which makes it difficult for the compositor to follow, and hence he consumes more time in making these alterations. This waste of time applies also to the reader, whose duty it is to see that the author's corrections have been properly effected.

It is also recommended that all old proofs bearing author's corrections or alterations be retained. They are sometimes necessary for the verification of charges, or in checking some presumed "error of the press," which has been discovered later stage.

On receiving a proof the first thing to be done is to read it through carefully, not *noticing the sense*,

The Proof-Reader's Marks Explained.

New par. or *n. p.* or [. Commence a fresh line or paragraph.

× A bad or battered letter.

ð Delete, expunge, or omit.

l. c. A capital or small capital to be changed to a lower-case or small letter.

Run on. An instruction to follow on previous matter and not to commence a new line.

| A space or quadrat to be pushed down.

⊙ A full-stop, or full-point, to be inserted.

□ The line to be indented one em of its own body.

Ꝺ A letter upside down, or turned round.

∟ Space to be reduced.

Rom. Change into roman.

Trs. Transpose a word or words.

ξ The types being crooked, to be straightened.

Cap. A lower-case letter to be altered to a capital, expressed also by three lines under, ☰.

⌒ The words or letters between this to be joined.

♯ A space to be inserted.

⋀ A caret mark.   Insert matter written in the margin.

w.f. A letter of a "wrong fount" to be changed.

Ital. Change into *italic*—sometimes indicated by a single underlining.

but searching for "letterals," or, in other words, seeing that every single word is spelt correctly. If sense and meaning be examined in the first place, the eyes get so accustomed to the words and their spelling that mistakes—even flagrant ones—are sometimes overlooked. Whatever else be wrong, a book *must* be spelt correctly!

Among many other desirable things it is important that an author should always verify in the proofs all extracts, references to dates, titles, and so forth.

When the first proof has been read and marked by the author, and he wishes to see it again, he should write " Revise " on the top left-hand corner, and return it to the printer, who will submit a " revise " to him with the corrections carried out. Should the corrections be few and the author not wish to see it again, he writes " Press " on the sheet, which means that no more alterations will be made by him, and that after the corrections have been effected by the compositor it can at once be printed. The final, or " press proof," is always retained by the printer for future reference in case of any dispute, and the author or editor should always preserve the intermediate proofs bearing corrections, in case of queries afterwards arising.

Printer's readers, styled " correctors of the press," are, as a rule, a very careful and painstaking body of men. Generally with practical experience, and sometimes a classical knowledge, they virtually sub-edit the MS. The queries they mark on proofs should always be *carefully* considered, as they frequently indicate an interpretation of the copy that may not have occurred to the author. Searching for an interpretation of his query may often show that the passage may be understood in two ways—one of which the author may not have thought about. Hence their queries *well* repay consideration.

What amount of printed matter will the MS. make—how many pages will it cover, in fact? This is not always an easy question to answer. No exact rules can be laid down ; manuscript copy varying so much in character of writing, and in the quantity of deletions and insertions. A practical man has frequently to spend much time and patience on manuscripts for estimation. Printers are frequently and astonishingly accurate in calculating most difficult manuscript.

It is not possible to explain in writing how to deal with intricate MSS. ; it requires experience and practical knowledge. One blank page for the beginning and ending of each chapter must be allowed on the average, and extra matter and footnotes, should there be either, must be considered.

If your copy is a fair one, open the MS. at ten different places, taken purely at random (they must not be selected in *any* way), and count the number of lines on each of the pages, and also the number of words in any one line (taken again at random), on each of the ten pages ; add together the number

of lines.   Strike out the last figure of the total,
and you have the average number of lines per
page ; then do the same with the words, and you
have their average number.   Multiply these two
together, and you have the number of words per
page ; multiply this by the number of pages, and
you will have the approximate number of words
in the whole.

Mark this number on the outside sheet, as a
guide to the publisher, and do not forget at the
same time to put your name and address, in case
it may get lost.

By the same method it is easy to find the number
of words in any printed book when, for instance,
it is desired to compare sizes.

A rough and ready way to find the average
quantity of English words contained in one square
inch of ordinary printed matter in "old style" type
will be to use the following table :

	Solid.	Thin leaded.	Thick leaded.
Great Primer	8	7	7
English	12	11	10
Pica	15	14	12
Small Pica	23	19	16
Long Primer	27	24	20
Bourgeois	32	28	24
Brevier	38	33	29
Minion	44	37	33
Nonpareil	59	47	40
Pearl	81	65	55

A reference to the various specimens of types

at the end of this volume and the analysis table on page 92 will further help to form an idea of the quantity contained in any given page, set in the other founts.

The headline for every page should be settled by the author himself. It is usual to have the short title of the work on the top of the left-hand page, and either the title of the chapter, or the subject-matter of the two pages open at the same time, on the top of the right-hand page. The former headline is useful in identifying and re-placing a leaf that may have been torn out, and the latter is of frequent use to the reader, and often a very great help in compiling an intelligible index.

It may be well to say a few words here about the Preface. It is the introductory address of the author, in which he explains the purpose and scope of his book. In these days of hurriedly-written newspaper reviews, it is useful to make the pre-face *thoroughly* explain the author's object in writing the book; for be it hinted to the budding author that in some cases this is the *only* part of the work read by the reviewer.

The "preliminary matter" is usually the last to be dealt with. The correct order in which it should appear at the commencement of English books—for this does not hold on the Continent—is half-title (a leaf to protect the full title from injury); title, of course bearing the date of pub-lication; dedication, almost obsolete now; preface, contents, and list of illustrations if there be any.

In a limited edition the certificate or guarantee of number printed should face either the half-title or title-page.

If the work has passed through many editions, a bibliographical list with the respective dates of issue is often, and usefully, placed facing or backing the title-page, if not already occupied with some other bibliographical detail. In this connection it is most important that the precise year of publication be expressed at the foot of the title-page. To omit the year or to postdate the issue is very misleading.

CHAPTER II

THE INDEX

LL works are the better for an Index, and its absence in those dealing with scientific matters is frequently noticed as a great fault by reviewers. The "Athenæum" nearly always gives credit to a volume which contains a good index, and points out the omission should it be a work requiring one.

In making an index, it is not enough for the indexer merely to understand the subject of the book, but he must understand the wants of the reader : two quite distinct things. The art of finding the correct title—or, as it is called, the "catchword"—under which to describe the thing indexed, must be combined with the knowledge that under that head, and no other, will the reader most probably look for it. Hence a specialist in the particular subject of which the book treats may not compile so valuable an index as one who, while knowing less of the subject, has had more experience in the ways of readers, and the catchwords they use.

A good index must be exhaustive ; must include the various "points" of a book ; must gather under one heading the same subjects ; must be concise, yet explicit ; must contain the subjects of chapters, and the smaller divisions, such as sections, not merely single words as they occur ; and must define each entry that occurs under the same title, so that the reader may turn at once to the desired page.

An index cannot be commenced until the sheets as finally printed are at hand, otherwise errors in pagination are sure to occur. Supposing the sheets are at hand, the best way to commence is to have an ordinary ruled copy-book, and to make each entry as it is decided upon, writing the catch-word somewhat more plainly than the subsequent definition, so as to catch the eye when turning back for reference, as is often necessary.

Between each entry leave one line blank for the subsequent cutting up and sorting which will be necessary.

As each entry is made, underline the word in-dexed in the text, if it is there, or write it in the margin if not, so that when the index proof comes to be checked with the sheets, the eye may readily catch the sought-for word.

In front of the desk, and visible without effort, should be kept the list of cross-references. This should be written up as each heading is decided upon, and selected from one or more possible synonyms. For instance, if " Printing " is the title selected and entered on the cross-reference sheet, there will be no subsequent re-arranging required from say such headings as " Book," " Caxton,"

" Fount," " Typography," for these will all be referred on the cross-reference sheet to " Printing."

Do not imagine that it is sufficient to select mere words as they occur in the text. Entries must be made for the contents of whole chapters, sections, and paragraphs. For the indexer must give the author credit for wanting to say some special thing in each subdivision of his work, and must similarly credit the intellectual reader with—having once found that particular subject dealt with—a desire to refer to it again, although pagination and all else concerning it has vanished from his mind.

When all the sheets have been extracted, and all the entries made in the copy-book—or it may be many copy-books—it then remains to separate the book into loose pages, and to cut with scissors along all the intermediate blank lines; then to sort the slips thus freed into alphabetical order; and then all slips with the same title in page order, commencing with the lowest. When this is done, to paste or gum them all on sheets of paper in proper order, and to revise them for the press, putting in cross-references from the sheet where a record of them has been kept, properly punctuating, eliminating duplicate headings by transferring page numbers, and otherwise giving the compositor as little trouble as possible when it comes into his hands.

The punctuation of an index may seem a simple matter, but it may be such as to make or mar it for a bibliographic eye. To make the catchword or heading of each entry prominent, it may be printed in a special fount, or even in *italic* or small capitals, or, if this be not desired—as it may involve extra expense—a good plan, which still throws up the heading a little, is to put a colon (:) after the first word. A comma should be put between the last word of an entry and the first figure of the page, and a semicolon between each entry under the same heading. Where there are several pages given to one reference, put a comma between each.

When the index proof comes from the printer it *must* be checked with the *pages of the book itself*, for who has not known the irritation produced by an incorrect page number in an index ? Many hours of labour will be saved in this dreary task if the word indexed has been—as recommended— underlined on the page itself at the time it was selected, and marginal notes made of anything not in the text.

CHAPTER III

Types and Margins

THE beauty of a volume is dependent on the selection of a suitable character of type. These "founts" of type may be broadly classified into three divisions, namely :

(*a*) The Old Face
(*b*) Revived Old Style Face
(*c*) The Modern Face

These three examples are given in large founts (double pica) to emphasize the difference in the character of the letters.

(*a*) The Old Face is occasionally used for bookwork, generally of an antiquarian character, the old-fashioned long ſ being sometimes used in conjunction with the ligatured letters, ſi ſl ff ſt ſh ſſi ſſl ſk ſb ct. This series was designed and cut by William Caslon, who flourished in the early part of the eighteenth century. It is closely modelled on the Dutch types used in the seventeenth century.

(*b*) The Revived Old Style is more generally used for bookwork, as a glance at most modern books will show. This volume is printed in this style, and in the Pica size, from Messrs. Miller and Richard's series, which was designed about the middle of the nineteenth century.

(*c*) The Modern Face is more in demand for newspapers, magazines, schoolbooks, scientific works, pamphlets, and so forth. This class of type faces was mostly created in the first half of the nineteenth century.

There are many other varieties of type, but they are mostly of a fanciful character, and not in good taste or in keeping with bookwork. However, the occasional use of **𝔟𝔩𝔞𝔠𝔨 𝔩𝔢𝔱𝔱𝔢𝔯**, *italic*, and a **bolder face** of type is permissible in order to give emphasis to certain passages. **This fatter face of type** is sometimes called "Clarendon," and occasionally "Egyptian." **This one is generally termed "Antique Roman," and has a pretty effect, especially with old style types.**

Fancy types need not be entirely rejected. Their characters are sometimes good, and their employment is appropriate for advertisements and works of a miscellaneous or commercial nature.

The types on the following page represent the "revived old style" in some of the different sizes in general use. The black impression at the beginning of each line represents the actual depth of the type-body employed in that particular line.

It should be remembered that pica is, when set solid, six lines to the inch. If this is taken as a standard the various other sizes, both smaller and larger, will in due time fix themselves on the mind.

Pearl is the name and size of the type shown here in this specimen page of old style types.

Nonpareil is the name and size of the type shown here in this specimen page of old

Minion is the name and size of the type shown here in this specimen page of

Brevier is the name and size of the type shown here in this specimen

Bourgeois is the name and size of the type shown here in this

Long Primer is the name and size of the type shown here in

Small Pica is the name and size of the type shown here

Pica is the name and size of the type shown here

English is the name and size of the type

Great Primer is the name and size

Double Pica is the name

2-line English is the

2-lineGreatPrimer

Canon is th

Each separate kind of type is made in many sizes, each size having a special name: that of the type used in this work is "Pica." The following table shows all the ordinary sizes for book work, with their approximate dimensions, and equivalents where they happen to be in proportion. There are of course larger sizes, but these lie rather outside our present scope.

Size.	Is half the size of	Lines to inch "solid."
Diamond	Bourgeois	17
Pearl	Long Primer	15
Ruby	Small Pica	14
Nonpareil	Pica	12
Minion	English	$10\frac{1}{8}$
Brevier	Two-line Brevier	$9\frac{1}{2}$
Bourgeois	Great Primer	$8\frac{1}{2}$
Long Primer	Paragon	$7\frac{1}{2}$
Small Pica	Double Pica	7
Pica	Two-line Pica	6
English	Two-line English	$5\frac{1}{4}$
Great Primer	Two-line Great Primer	$4\frac{1}{4}$
Paragon	Two-line Paragon	$3\frac{3}{4}$
Double Pica	Two-line Double Pica	$3\frac{1}{2}$

This table is based on the old system of type measurement. The American system of type bodies is gradually coming into use here. It is measured by points, taking pica $= 12$ points, or roughly 72 points to the inch. This innovation is a good one, as each size of type bears a definite ratio to other sizes, whereas the former custom of the different English founders resulted in chaos, for, as a rule, no two founts of the same body made by different founders could be used together.

This is an example of the point system, which speaks for itself:

	Points			Points
Diamond	= 4½	*is half of*	Bourgeois	= 9
Pearl	= 5	„	Long Primer	= 10
Ruby	= 5½	„	Small Pica	= 11
Nonpareil	= 6	„	Pica	= 12
Minion	= 7	„	English	= 14
Brevier	= 8	„	Two-line Brevier	= 16
Bourgeois	= 9	„	Great Primer	= 18
Long Primer	= 10	„	Paragon	= 20
Small Pica	= 11	„	Double Pica	= 22
Pica	= 12	„	Two-line Pica	= 24
English	= 14	„	Two-line English	= 28
Great Primer	= 18	„	Two-line Great Primer	= 36

It may be as well here to explain the unit of measurement which the printer employs, and has indeed employed since the time of Caxton. It should be thoroughly understood, as it is frequently referred to in printing matters.

Really the "em" ▌ is but the name for the unit which represents the actual square of the side of any particular body, and has no connection with the letter "m" excepting that it is sometimes thus abbreviated. An "en" ▌ is the same depth precisely, but half the width of an "em," so two *ens* ▌ make one *em* ▌ This pica "em" is the standard adopted for governing the measure or width of type matter. The wages value of any page is obtained by measuring the actual length and width in ems of that fount in which the volume or work is composed, this being doubled to obtain the *ens*, *e.g.*, $50 \times 20 = 1,000 \times 2 = 2,000$. This gives the number of letters in a page—the *en* being considered the average thickness of the twenty-six letters of the alphabet. For example, supposing the twenty-six letters of the lower-case roman alphabet (a to z) were set up in the composing stick, the total length of the complete alphabet should not be less than twelve *ems* of its own body; more often it is thirteen or fourteen ems. If less than twelve ems it is a "thin" fount, and the compositors are paid extra for the additional work it entails.

That there are six pica ems to the inch should be remembered. As an illustration : the width of this page is twenty-one pica ems. Now $\frac{21}{6} = 3\frac{1}{2}$; therefore the print on the page is three and a half inches wide, which any rule will show it to be.

Lines of type are frequently separated by the insertion of thin strips of lead : "solid" type is when set without "leads." This text is set up "thin leaded." Forty-eight "thin leads" go to one inch, and two are equal to one "thick lead." Therefore twenty-four "thick leads" are equal to an inch, and consequently four to the pica.

By means of leading a volume may be spun out to almost any number of pages, and books are even double or treble thick-leaded all through. Opinions differ as to the appearance of leaded and

non-leaded matter.   Undoubtedly a page of type
set quite close looks pretty as a whole, but for
comfort in reading, unless the type is fairly large
and the page not too wide, the eyes travel more
easily from the end of one line to the beginning
of the next if it be leaded.   In the larger dictionaries and encyclopædias the difficulty of reading
across a wide page of small print is obviated by
dividing the pages into two, three, or more columns.

Where a reprint of a book is expected—as for
a second edition—the expense of re-setting all the
type may be saved by various processes.   The
principle of them all is, to take a mould of the
type in some material from which a metal impress
may be obtained forthwith or at any future time.
This impress takes the place of the original type,
and is printed from with varying results, the exact
degree of quality being dependent on the process
employed.

In moulding by the patent or paper (papier-
maché) process, papier-maché moulds are formed
by placing several sheets of prepared paper together, pasted with a special composition.   This,
after being moistened, is laid on the surface of the
type and then beaten with a large brush.   It thus
forms a "matrix," which is dried by artificial means.
These moulds are then stored.   When required,
melted metal is poured on them, and in the "stereotype" resulting each page is faithfully reproduced
as in the original type.   With care the results
obtained in printing are fairly good.   This is an

inexpensive method, as these moulds need not be stereotyped until they are required. Daily newspapers are all produced by means of this plan.

A better process is the plaster, but now almost obsolete in practice. In this the matrix is formed with plaster poured over the surface of the type. This is afterwards baked, and the metal poured into it, thus giving a reproduction. This method is more satisfactory as giving a sharper and more even stereotype, but it is slower and more expensive. Music type is nearly always stereotyped by this process.

Electrotyping is the art of duplicating by an electro-deposit of copper from a mould made in wax, which forms a mere filmy shell, afterwards backed up with type-metal to give it the requisite thickness and strength. This is more durable, but costs rather more than the plaster stereotype, which it has largely superseded. It is well adapted for works that have to be reprinted many times, because, the face being harder, a larger number of impressions are given with less wear and tear. It is always used for duplicating woodcuts, a careful electrotype being almost equal to the original block from which it is made. If woodcuts are to be preserved they should be electrotyped, and prints made only from the duplicates, the originals not being used, and carefully preserved. When worn, a fresh electrotype can always be readily taken.

If a work is likely to run into another edition and

it becomes necessary to correct the matter somewhat extensively, some arrangement with the
printer to keep the type standing is usual, because
alterations in stereotype- or electrotype-plates are
very expensive to make. Such type kept to
special order is generally subject to a nominal
rental based on a fair interest on the value of the
material locked up for the time being.

It will be seen from this that the paper process
allows of tentative moulds being taken in the first
place, and, if they are never used afterwards, this
first cost is not of great moment. If required at
some later date, these moulds are equally good for
casting from, provided they have been taken good
care of. In the plaster-stereotyping and electrotyping instances the plates must be made forthwith,
because these moulds in either case could not be
stocked without injury.

We now approach another important feature in
the appearance of a well-printed book.

Margin is a matter to be studied. To place the
print in the centre of the paper is wrong in principle, and to be deprecated. If we look at a book
printed in this fashion, it is apparent to the book-
lover that something is amiss; for by an optical
illusion its pages have the appearance of having
more margin on the inner and top edges than on
the outer and lower margins.

To remedy this it is therefore necessary to have
more margin on the outer than the inner side of
a page, called respectively the "fore-edge" and

"back"; and less at the top, or "head," than at the bottom, or "tail."

In fact, the two facing pages of the open book must both be taken into consideration at the same time.

Apart from this, the larger amount of paper on the fore-edge and tail serves a double purpose. It allows of subsequent rebinding and cutting; and it also allows room for annotation. A reference to some of the best printed books of the past will show that this margin was much used in olden times for this purpose. In modern times the Kelmscott Press books may be cited as an instance, though perhaps a little exaggerated. It is also useful, as there is more wear and tear on these portions of a book. Indeed, books may be seen that have had their fore-edge actually worn away in places by incessant fingering until they are one-eighth of an inch, or more, narrower than they were originally.

The proportion of margin depends upon the size of the book: there must be a gradual increase from a sextodecimo to a folio.

In an *édition de luxe* it is well not to make the difference in size too extravagant, though no definite rules in this matter can be laid down.

Supposing a book is printed in the revived old style type on a machine paper, it is quite permissible to print the large paper copies on a handmade paper.

Sometimes, where the difference in size between

two editions is not very great, and the size happens to be quarto, the inner and top margins are not altered. In this case the extra paper would fall on the fore-edge and tail of the book. This plan obviates the expense of altering margins of type pages and saves the cost of a fresh making-ready on the press.

These sizes are suggested for the difference between small and large paper editions.

OCTAVOS.

Foolscap $6\frac{3}{4} \times 4\frac{1}{4}$ *may become* Crown $7\frac{1}{2} \times 5$ inches.
Crown $7\frac{1}{2} \times 5$ „   „   Demy $8\frac{3}{4} \times 5\frac{5}{8}$
Post 8×5 „   „   Medium $9\frac{1}{2} \times 6$
Demy $8\frac{3}{4} \times 5\frac{5}{8}$ „   „   Royal $10 \times 6\frac{1}{4}$
Medium $9\frac{1}{2} \times 6$ „   „   Super Royal $10\frac{1}{4} \times 6\frac{7}{8}$
Royal $10 \times 6\frac{1}{4}$ „   „   Imperial $11 \times 7\frac{1}{2}$

QUARTOS.

Foolscap $8\frac{1}{2} \times 6\frac{3}{4}$ *may become* Crown $10 \times 7\frac{1}{2}$ inches.
Crown $10 \times 7\frac{1}{2}$ „   „   Demy $11\frac{1}{4} \times 8\frac{3}{4}$
Post 10×8 „   „   Medium $12 \times 9\frac{1}{2}$
Demy $11\frac{1}{4} \times 8\frac{3}{4}$ „   „   Royal $12\frac{1}{2} \times 10$
Medium $12 \times 9\frac{1}{2}$ „   „   Super Royal $13\frac{3}{4} \times 10\frac{1}{4}$
Royal $12\frac{1}{2} \times 10$ „   „   Imperial 15×11

CHAPTER IV

METHODS OF ILLUSTRATION

T now becomes necessary to devote some attention to what is very often the most important feature where a modern book is concerned —the illustrations.

Within the last few years illustrated books have become more and more frequent, until at the present time very few books are published without some kind of illustration, or attempt at least, at typographical decoration. The facility with which illustrations can be produced is largely responsible for this tendency : on the other hand, the demand for "pictures" in a book has undoubtedly stimulated the development of modern methods of engraving until the variety of processes available for the purpose is positively bewildering.

In the selection of the mode of illustration, one must be guided by whether the designs are original or whether the pictures are mere reproductions of old subjects. If the former, the drawings can be generally adapted to the requirements of the particular process to be employed, the precise method being regulated by the total expense to be incurred ; whereas, in the case of reproductions, the choice would naturally be more limited. Nowadays nearly all illustrations are mechanically

D

produced, and the actual cost of making any blocks or plates may be taken in the following order : line process, half-tone process, collotype and other photo-mechanical gelatine methods, and, lastly, photogravure as the most expensive.   It must be remembered, too, that the first two being relief processes, the blocks may be incorporated with type matter in printing, but the last two methods necessitate quite separate and distinct printings from letterpress and are best adapted for inserted plates in a volume.

When the printed book succeeded the written and illuminated manuscript its pages were undoubtedly printed from a single block upon which had been engraved in reverse relief the characters of the required lettering.   And, as such books were mainly of a devotional kind, masses or service books predominating, it was the custom to supplement the letterpress matter with a rude outline design.   These were engraved on small selected planks of straight-grained pear or sycamore wood : the lines were cut by means of a knife and followed the direction of the grain of the wood, in contradistinction to the later method of wood engraving, where the blocks are cut upon the end of the grain.

Such a method naturally did not afford much scope for the engraver, but all the extant examples of early wood engraving bear remarkable testimony to the wonderful power and resource of their designers.   When the use of movable types

for printing letterpress became general, blocks
were no longer required, and woodcut illustration
fell into disuse. But simultaneously with the
introduction of block-printing there occurred a
very general extension of the practice of the art
of engraving in the sense in which that term has
been so universally employed.

Such work consists in engraving a design upon
the surface of a smooth plate of metal with a burin
or graver. The engraved plate is inked; the
surface wiped so as to leave only ink in the incised lines; then an impression is taken on soft
paper in a roller press. With proper attention to
the amount and quality of pressure applied, and a
judicious selection of an appropriate paper and ink,
engraved plates give really fine artistic results.
And as line engraving was capable of such results,
it was during the seventeenth and eighteenth
centuries, when books were not many, and when
illustrated books formed only a small proportion
of the total output, the method most generally
adopted. Not that illustrations were numerous:
the fact that they involved a separate printing and
were divorced from the letterpress effectually pre-
vented their extended use, and generally speaking
they were limited either to a decorative title-page
or frontispiece.

Such briefly was the condition of things until
the end of the eighteenth century: with the dawn of
the nineteenth a new era begins, and illustration
becomes a more important feature in books than

previously. The invention of the art of lithography by Senefelder furnished the artist with a
fresh method, and, although open to the objection
already urged against line engraving, the necessity
for a separate printing did not prove altogether
fatal to the use of lithography for book illustration. Commonly regarded as a mysterious art, lithography is really a very simple affair, and is based
upon the power of certain kinds of mineral matter
to absorb fatty organic substances. A smooth-
surfaced piece of porous carboniferous limestone is
selected, and the opposite sides are ground so as to
form a fairly uniform and flat bed of stone; one
face is polished, and upon this the artist makes his
drawing with a greasy pigment. When the design
is finished it is usual to give a slight acid bath, or
" etch the stone," as it is termed, for the purpose
of imprisoning the greasy pigment within the
minute pores of the surface of the stone. If the
stone be damped and then rolled up with an
elastic roller charged with a greasy printing ink,
that ink will adhere to the design, while the damp
stone will repel it. The stone can then be printed
by passing it through a press fitted with a scraper.

Before passing from this short consideration of
the lithographic art, it may be useful to note that
when a slightly grained instead of a polished stone
is used, no more perfect method exists for faithfully
reproducing in the printed impression the real
character of a drawing executed in chalk or pencil,
and that, by reason of the delicacy and subtlety

of the tints which can be printed from stone, lithography is extensively employed in colour-printing.

The early part of the nineteenth century saw the revival of wood engraving, and, we may add, the end of that same century its decline. When the mediæval German and Fleming worked upon wood they cut their designs as already stated upon a longitudinal plank, and their opportunities for adequate expression of the intention of their designs were limited accordingly. But Bewick, his contemporaries and pupils, were not content with these restricted facilities : they were familiar with the work of several generations of line engravers, and realized that a much wider field was open to them if they could treat their blocks as line engravers treated their plates. Accordingly they employed a hard wood and engraved their blocks on the end of the grain. These transverse sections were trimmed and surfaced, one face being finely polished. Upon this the artist's design was drawn, and the picture made no longer with a knife but with a burin.

The task of the wood engraver was not quite so simple as that of his brother craftsman upon metal. While the latter was required to plough the surface of his plate to produce his line, and inflection could be obtained by merely varying the pressure which he exerted, and so making a deep and wide cut or a shallow and thin one, the wood engraver had to leave his line alone, and cut out

what are known as the "whites," or the blank
spaces between the lines.

For fully half a century the superiority of wood
engraving for the purpose of general book illustration was unchallenged. Artists of repute became
book illustrators, but few of them had been trained
as engravers or were willing to undertake the
drudgery of such training, and it frequently
happened that the artist, being dependent upon
the engraver for the translation of his design, and
the drawing being destroyed during the progress
of the work, perfeƈt results were not always forth-
coming. Photography was then employed to assist
the artist, and instead of drawing direƈtly upon the
wood-block he was enabled to make an independent
drawing and have it transferred to the surface of
the block, which had been specially sensitized for
the purpose. Wood engraving was a slow process ;
both artist and engraver had to be employed—and
paid. The cost of produƈtion was considerable,
and if illustrations were to be extensively used
some cheaper method of engraving must be found.
Now, the lithographers had ascertained by praƈtical
experience that it was possible to use thin plates of
polished zinc in the place of the ordinary lithographic stone. Transfers from the stone were
made ; they were laid down on zinc plates and
printed from with ease and certainty. From the
substitution of zinc plates for lithographic stones, a
single step sufficed to convert them into relief blocks
capable of being printed at a letterpress machine.

All that was required was to draw upon the zinc with a greasy pigment, or one containing a resisting varnish, and then to etch the plate with acid. The whites of the design were thus bitten away, and the lines, having been protected by the varnish from the action of the acid, were untouched and remained in relief. When mounted upon a wooden or metal support of sufficient thickness, the plate could be imposed with type and printed in the ordinary way.

We have already seen that the aid of photography was invoked by the wood engraver; it was destined to render still more important service to the process engraver. Instead of drawing directly upon the metal, the zincographer makes a reversed negative from his drawing, and having sensitized the surface of his plate proceeds to print the negative upon it. This is effected by covering the zinc plate with a thin coating of albumen, in which potassium bichromate has been dissolved. When dry the negative is exposed in contact to the action of light, and it is found that the physical condition of the sensitized albumen undergoes an important change. Where the light has penetrated the negative, the albumen has been rendered insoluble in water; where, on the contrary, the dense film of the negative prevents the passage of light, there is no alteration in the condition of the albumen. After rolling up with a lithographic ink the plate can be washed and the unprinted albumen dissolved away, the remaining portion, acted upon by light corresponding with the lines of the design, being undisturbed. The plate is then etched, and when sufficient relief is obtained mounted and printed from in the manner already described. Modified in various particulars and improved in detail this is the ordinary line process now in common use. Where a drawing is prepared with due regard to photographic requirements it is an excellent method of obtaining at very small cost an efficient and faithful reproduction. A subject that would have formerly cost several pounds if engraved on wood, can be reproduced by line process for a few shillings, the rate for the finest work of this class not exceeding sixpence per square inch, while in a great many instances it is much lower.

It must not be imagined, however, that line process will satisfactorily reproduce any drawing, although such a belief is commonly but erroneously entertained. The drawing must be made in a suitable manner; it must express everything the artist intends to convey, and, as a good photograph is an essential preliminary, it must be made in clear, firm, definite black lines. There must be no question as to colour, otherwise over-exposure in the negative cannot be avoided, and this results in thickened and distorted lines, or, on the other hand, in their becoming broken and rotten in the reproduction. The drawing should be rather hard; all the tone is to be obtained by cross-hatching or by tints made up of line; no wash or pencil work is admissible. Sometimes it is advantageous to make it somewhat larger in proportion than the resulting block, but when this is done the artist must not be tempted, because he has a larger surface to cover, to put more work upon his design than would be required for a reproduction to scale. Simplicity is desirable, and the most effective pen drawings are generally those which are made with the least effort.

The zincographic line process is very rapid in operation. Using artificial light and labour-saving contrivances in the various stages of its manufacture, a block can be completed in a very few hours; so quickly, indeed, that this process is extensively employed for daily newspaper purposes, where the entire preparation of the paper has to be completed between sunset and sunrise.

Another process in which the block is produced by swelling a photographic print made upon a gelatine film, so as to enable a cast of the lines to be obtained in relief, was for some time extensively used in America as well as in this country. Except in the case of originals where the colour is imperfect, or for reproductions from old and stained prints of existing engravings, it possesses no advantage over the ordinary zinc method, and being more complicated in working its use has almost entirely died out.

Artists accustomed to draw upon wood were unfettered as to technique. Sometimes they chose to indicate the precise treatment the engraver was to adopt when interpreting a design, but very fre-

quently they were content to make a wash drawing on the wood-block, and left the engraver
to use his own discretion in translating the monochrome into a line engraving, for it must be
remembered that for letterpress printing a definite
texture of lines or dots must exist. There is a
level surface exposed to pressure, and, except as
modified by the making-ready, the amount and
distribution of colour in the design can only be
expressed by means of lines and dots of different
sizes, shapes, and directions. Men familiar with
line drawing were quite at home when called upon
to produce drawings for photographic reproduction,
but a larger and equally capable class of illustrators
were at a disadvantage inasmuch as they lacked
the ability to express tone properly by means of
line. So the photographers turned their attention
to perfecting some arrangement whereby wash or
monochrome drawing should be made available for
printing at letterpress, and the solution of the
problem resulted in what is known as the half-tone
process, the most extensively used of any existing
method of illustration.

The half-tone engraver does for the drawing in
flat tint what the draughtsman in line does for
himself, and his function is somewhat akin to that
of the wood engraver engaged in cutting tints.
In point of fact the half-tone operator converts an
indefinite tint, whether in wash or pencil, or the
tone of an ordinary photographic print, incapable
as it stands of direct expression at the letterpress

machine, into a texture of dots and points which can be readily printed from.

This is accomplished by very similar methods to those of the ordinary line process. There is, indeed, a close analogy between them, the only radical difference being found in the negative. A negative from an outline drawing will obviously represent that drawing exactly, the lines will appear as transparent replicas of those in the drawing, and the colour of the paper will be represented by the opaque film of the negative. In the case of a monochrome it has to be replaced by one made with a screen interposed between the drawing and the sensitive plate. The screen is a very fine piece of optical apparatus. It is composed of two sheets of plate glass absolutely free from flaws or defects of any description whatever. These are ruled by means of delicate machinery fitted with movements capable of exact mathematical adjustment so as to insure uniformity in the width both of the line itself and the spaces between the lines. The ruling on each generally follows the direction of the diagonal, and the two sheets are secured face to face and hermetically sealed. The sealing material is opaquely coloured, and when viewed against a luminous background the screen is seen to be composed of minute squares. The number of lines to the inch and the ratio between the width of line and intervening space vary. Originally screens of eighty or one hundred lines to the inch were employed, now screens of one hundred and fifty up to two hundred lines to the inch are common, and even finer screens are used where the conditions will permit of the most careful printing. When inserted in the camera in front of the sensitive plate the action of the screen is to intercept very much of the transmitted light from the copy, and to break up the image into that mass of dots and points, which, whether conspicuous or almost imperceptible, is always present in a half-tone engraving. Having secured the negative, the later stages of the production of a half-tone block are similar to those already described in connection with line blocks. Copper has largely replaced zinc as the material used, and the various stages of re-biting require greater deftness on the part of the operator than the corresponding steps in making a line block.

Before entirely leaving the subject of photography as applied to either letterpress or lithographic printing, a few words are necessary on the subject of colour printing, and also as to those photo-mechanical methods of printing which are sometimes used in connection with book illustration.

Colour printing involves a number of separate blocks or stones for one subject, the number varying with the number of colours to be used. The lithographer selects from his design the appropriate colours, and, having drawn the key or general outline, he lays down a number of transfers on to separate stones. On one he will draw in so much of the tint as is necessary to obtain, say, the yellow,

and on another what is required to give the blue,
and on another the violet, and so on. Each one
of course is treated with sufficient inflection to
convey the different strengths of colour, and again
separate stones are provided for such intermediate
tints as cannot very well be secured by a combina-
tion of any other colours used. All these transfers
being laid down from one key they can be printed
in succession in perfect register, and so the colour
print is gradually built up.

Where a long run is required, some economy is
found in employing relief blocks instead of lithographic stones, or again it is sometimes advantageous to combine the two methods, and print
part of the work from stone and the rest from relief
blocks. The increasing tendency to produce
colour work by letterpress has lately contributed
to an important development of the photographic
half-tone process, which is generally known as
"three-colour work." The researches of Ives and
others in the field of photographic optics have
demonstrated that it is possible to construct photographic positives which will discriminate natural
colours.

The photographer does this by making negatives
in register on specially prepared sensitive plates
so arranged that each one shall automatically select
only a sympathetic colour and reject any other.
In this way a negative may be obtained from any
object which shall reproduce only so much of it
as is coloured yellow, another shall reproduce

the blue, and another the purple. If half-tone blocks are made from these, and are printed in pigments corresponding as closely as possible with the colours selected by the respective negative filters, a fairly satisfactory result may be obtained. It is clear, however, that any such result is an approximation only, and its success depends largely upon the character of the subject to be reproduced. Natural objects as a rule present fewer difficulties than paintings or drawings in colour.

A very brief reference to the photo-mechanical processes will suffice. They are numerous, and for fidelity of reproduction are valuable, but they involve separate printing, and in some cases this is a costly matter. The most important are the group of collotype processes, which are known by a variety of names. A collotype may be described as a mechanical print from a chemically prepared surface, and is in effect a lithograph printed from a gelatine film. In this country climatic changes are so frequent and sudden that it is difficult to rely upon the behaviour of gelatine, which is largely affected by variations of temperature, and by the amount of moisture present in the atmosphere. Very fine granulation can be employed, and therefore a collotype print is capable of expressing the most delicate textures and the lightest tints.

It only remains now to mention the group of illustrative methods known as intaglio or incised processes. Line engraving upon copper has been already referred to. A later development introduced the use of steel instead of copper plates, and a more delicate style of engraving became popular. During the earlier part of the last century, line and stipple engravings were used for book illustration in the case of sumptuous editions, but have now almost entirely died out. The revival of copper etching dates from the decline of line engraving. For the artist who is expert in the control of his treatment of line, no method can be simpler or more effective. Having covered a polished copperplate with a resist varnish, he draws in reverse with a sharp point the lines of his design, revealing the metal: he then proceeds to etch the plate, generally using a retarding mordant such as perchloride of iron. Not only can the width of line be varied, but its depth can also be regulated by re-covering the plate and re-biting those portions of the design which need strengthening.

Much more restricted in its application to book illustration is the mezzotinter's art. It is a complicated process to produce a mezzotint plate, and when done the number of perfect impressions that can be relied upon is not great. A copperplate is worked upon by a tool known as a "rocker," which raises a burr like velvet-pile. The engraving is made with a scraper, the burr is reduced in height for the middle tones, and is altogether removed for the high lights of the subject, which are represented by the smooth metal.

The plate is inked and printed in the same manner as a line copperplate, but the tint obtained by the rocking is so full and deep, and of such a varied character, that a print from a mezzotint plate always presents a rich appearance, and possesses a quality unobtainable in any other way.

The fact that every print from a copperplate involves a large amount of manual manipulation insures variety, and the introduction among the illustrations of a book of at least one printed from a plate enables it to claim a higher place among the season's editions than is allotted to others. Hence the need for a cheap and speedy method of making copperplate illustrations, which has been satisfied by the introduction of photogravure.

In connection with relief work gelatine surfaces for electrotyping purposes have already been mentioned. The use of undulating gelatine films in conjunction with resin for granulating the plate gives the process of photogravure.

A negative of the subject is made in the usual manner, and from this a reversed glass positive is printed. A carbon print is then made, which is laid down on a copperplate already covered with finely powdered resin. The undulations in the carbon film corresponding with the gradations of light and shade in the subject regulate the time required for a mordant to penetrate to the surface of the copperplate beneath, and permit of the more immediate action of the acid upon those parts where the carbon film is thinnest. These correspond with the shadows, while the denser film indicating the lights of the subject does not permit of much, if any, chemical action. The printing texture is secured by the powdered resin, the separate grains of which prevent the uninterrupted action of the mordant and granulate the bitten area.

Although not a particularly cheap process photogravure is an efficient and comprehensive method of securing artistic results in the way of book illustration, and for the reproduction of paintings it is unsurpassed by any of the mechanical processes. It is not unusual for us to be told that these may be dismissed as unworthy of consideration from that point of view which insists upon the individuality of the craftsman as the only criterion of artistic excellence, and photogravure has consequently received less attention than it deserves, the circumstance that much of the beauty of the finished product depends upon the skill of the retoucher being conveniently ignored. In practice the plate which requires little or no retouching is the one which soonest fails in printing.

This closes our review of the processes available for purposes of illustration. The sketch is necessarily incomplete—it cannot pretend to be more. It aims only at giving information which will aid an inquiring reader in his search for more.

E

CHAPTER V

PAPERS

AVING selected an appropriate type, and considered the illustrations, if a picture-book, the next thing is the question of Paper, of which there is an almost infinite variety.

In its selection the nature of the work must be constantly borne in mind. To put an old-faced type on machine paper, or a modern-faced on one made by hand, is not generally appropriate. To be consistent, it is best to print old-faced type on hand-made paper, or paper of an antique character; and most certainly modern-faced type on machine paper. The intermediate series of type faces—the revived old style—may, however, without offence to the most critical, be employed on either kind of paper.

All papers are primarily divided into two classes: the "hand-made" and the "machine-made." And each of these may be either "laid" or "wove." The hand-made may generally be recognized in the full size of sheet by having all round a raw, ragged, or rough edge—called the "deckle"—and usually by the right side being darker than the wrong. The machine-made papers have smooth, cut, or even edges, except imitation antiques, when they may have one, or two, or even four rough edges. In the last case they are machine-made in a mould, and are apt to deceive most persons. These papers as a rule are darker on the wrong side than on the right. The laid papers are also easily identified by the wire marks or water lines, which are rendered more visible when a sheet, or part of a sheet, is held up to the light. The wove papers lack such lines. Both kinds may, however, be found water-marked with some design or trade emblem.

Machine-made papers are made in a very great number of varieties : not only in shade of colour, but in style and quality ; this latter being largely dependent upon the amount of rag. Hand-made paper is desirable where durability and quality are sought, its texture being stronger, and its properties more lasting. Hand-made papers stand an equal strain in any direction, machine-made papers in one direction only. This can be tested by tearing a small square piece of paper and floating it on water. The hand-made will turn up on all four sides, and the machine-made only on two.

The substance of paper is regulated to a given weight per ream. For instance, the paper on which this book is printed is 32lb. demy, 516 sheets to the ream, and is a paper of the machine-made antique laid character. In selecting a paper that is of a thin substance, care should be taken to see that it is fairly opaque.

The principal sizes of machine-made printing papers measure in inches :

Foolscap	17 × 13½
Crown	20 × 15
Post	20 × 16
Demy	22½ × 17½
Medium	24 × 19
Double Pott	25 × 15½
Royal	25 × 20
Double Foolscap . . .	27 × 17
Super Royal	27½ × 20½
Double Crown	30 × 20
Imperial	30 × 22
Double Post	32 × 20
Columbia	34½ × 23½
Atlas	36 × 26

Hand-made printing papers may vary slightly.

Most of these papers are made in the double or quadruple sizes, because the modern fashion is to print on machines of larger capacity, for the twofold object of expedition and cheapness.

Very smooth or highly calendered papers are only recommended where the illustrations in the text absolutely require them, especially if these illustrations are of the half-tone nature; hand-made, or papers with a medium surface, being only adapted for printing illustrations of a purely outline character.

If possible, it is better to make separate plates of all illustrations, so that a good printing paper of ordinary finish may be employed for the letterpress portion of the work, these separate plates being afterwards inserted in their proper places by the binder.

A word may be said here about the so-called "art papers," which are but coated with a material that contains a very large proportion of clay. These papers certainly give the best results for half-tone cuts, but they are not recommended generally if a suitable super-calendered paper can be used instead. The loading of these papers adds considerably to the weight of the volume, and the dazzling glare of such papers renders them most uncomfortable and trying to the eyes in reading.

Other papers to be on the guard against are some of those of an advertised light-weight character. In all these there is an entire absence of strength or substance, and there is a great tendency in some of the cheaper kinds of these papers to disintegrate in the mere handling of the sheets in printing.

As regards the cost of papers, the average quality of hand-made is approximately about three times the value of machine-made—Whatman paper being a little dearer : say four times the value of a good quality of machine-made. That used by the late William Morris for his Kelmscott Press productions was even dearer. In limited editions of a work the total amount of paper used is so small that the price is not worth much consideration. For this reason it is advisable to use the best.

A ream of writing or hand-made paper usually consists of twenty quires, containing twenty-four sheets, or 480 in all; but machine-made paper generally contains 516 sheets (twenty-one and a half quires), termed "printers' reams." As long numbers are mostly printed on these papers, each ream, allowing for waste and spoilage, thus gives something more than 500 perfect copies.

Vellum is occasionally used for very special copies of a choice work, but its first cost and the subsequent trouble and expense in printing render it truly an *édition de luxe*. Nowadays it is somewhat difficult to obtain that material uniform in colour, thickness, and flexibility.

A substitute for vellum which has come into use during the past few years is the Japanese hand-made vellum paper. It is almost untearable, and its beautifully even and smooth surface is capable of receiving the finest impression. So much so, that it is largely used for printing engravings and etchings. Its cost as compared with real vellum is small, and not very much more than the best English hand-made rag paper. This paper is admirably adapted for children's toy-books, and also for sheet music, which has, as a rule, a bad habit of soon parting at the folds.

One objection, however, to the Japanese paper is that it is not easily cleaned should it become fingered, as its surface becomes rough in the process of cleaning.

CHAPTER VI

THE SIZES OF BOOKS

T is a difficult matter sometimes, even for the bibliophile, to discriminate between the various sizes of Books, but the rules here laid down will be found useful and generally correct. The present day custom of making books of various odd or irregular sizes, however, is apt to increase the difficulty.

Books are defined respectively as folio (2°), quarto (4to), octavo (8vo), duodecimo (12mo), sextodecimo (16mo), octodecimo (18mo), vigesimo-quarto (24mo), trigesimo-secundo (32mo), etc. These terms are founded upon the number of times a sheet is folded; for instance, a folio sheet would form two *leaves*, a quarto four, and so on. Sometimes it is difficult to distinguish, say, an octavo from a quarto; but if it is printed on a hand-made laid paper, the water-lines that run at intervals of one to two inches through the sheet (not to be confused with the wire-marks of the sheet, numbering usually eight or more to the inch) will mostly determine this. This rule should also apply to machine-made papers if the paper-maker knows his business. The signatures or letters placed at the foot of the first, and sometimes also the third page, serve as another guide to identification.

	Abbreviated to	Pages to one sheet.	Waterlines in hand-made.
Folio	Fo.	4	vertical
Quarto	4to	8	horizontal
Octavo	8vo	16	vertical
Duodecimo	12mo	24	horizontal
Sextodecimo	16mo	32	horizontal
Octodecimo	18mo	36	vertical
Vigesimo-quarto	24mo	48	vertical
Trigesimo-secundo	32mo	64	vertical

Books with uncut or merely trimmed edges should measure in inches :

	Octavo.			Quarto.	
Pott	$6\frac{1}{4}$ × $3\frac{7}{8}$	. . .	$7\frac{3}{4}$ ×	$6\frac{1}{4}$
Foolscap . . .	$6\frac{3}{4}$ × $4\frac{1}{4}$	. . .	$8\frac{1}{2}$ ×	$6\frac{3}{4}$
Crown . . .	$7\frac{1}{2}$ × 5	. . .	10 ×	$7\frac{1}{2}$
Post	8 × 5	. . .	10 ×	8
Demy . . .	$8\frac{3}{4}$ × $5\frac{5}{8}$	. . .	$11\frac{1}{4}$ ×	$8\frac{3}{4}$
Medium . . .	$9\frac{1}{2}$ × 6	. . .	12 ×	$9\frac{1}{2}$
Royal . . .	10 × $6\frac{1}{4}$	. . .	$12\frac{1}{2}$ ×	10
Super Royal .	$10\frac{1}{4}$ × $6\frac{7}{8}$	. . .	$13\frac{3}{4}$ ×	$10\frac{1}{4}$
Imperial . . .	11 × $7\frac{1}{2}$	. . .	15 ×	11

For books with cut edges, deduct a quarter of an inch in height, and rather less in width. If the book has been bound more than once, a greater deduction must of course be made.

There is not always a clear understanding as to the terms used in connection with the treatment of edges.

"Uncut edges" does not necessarily mean that they have not been opened with the ordinary hand paper-knife, but simply that the book has not been cut down by machine, a method which sometimes sadly mars the appearance of a book. When the edges are absolutely untouched, it is perhaps better to say " unopened."

" Trimmed edges " means that the heads have been left untouched and the fore-edge and tail merely trimmed sufficiently to make them tidy.

" Cut edges " are those cut perfectly smooth with a machine on three sides, and possibly—even probably—with a total disregard to the margins, perhaps facilitated by the bad margins of the printer in the first instance.

The principal use of signatures at the foot of the first page of a sheet is to guide the binder in folding; they also save the printer the trouble of referring to the pagination.

The letters of the alphabet are used as signatures, rarely figures, omitting J, V, W (evidently a survival of the days when Latin was the general language used in printing), and reserving A for the " preliminary " matter. If this preliminary matter exceeds a sheet, the signatures are continued with the small letters b, c, d, e, and so forth, technically called " lower case " letters, which may be either in roman or *italic*, as distinct from capitals or small capitals. Supposing the text of a volume exhausts the alphabet, the letters are duplicated as AA, BB, CC, or 2A, 2B, 2C, and so on.

Occasionally the third page of a sheet bears a subsidiary signature, marked B 2, C 2, D 2, etc., according to the signature on the first page. This is only requisite in such sizes of books as duodecimo or octodecimo, where a sheet cannot be properly folded without first cutting off and insetting a small section within the larger: this second signature indicating its position and acting as a check on its proper sheet.

CHAPTER VII

BINDING

INDING is the last stage in the production of a Book, and the question arises—should the book have a temporary, or a permanent, binding? Paper or cloth suffices for the former, but leather is necessary for the latter.

Taking the temporary binding first: it is important, if this is merely a tentative binding, that the edges should *not* be cut, but the binder or the owner should open it carefully with a knife, otherwise its size will be too small for the final and permanent covering.

There are many ways of doing up books temporarily. They may be in loose paper wrappers, or in cloth, which is generally called publisher's binding, or "case work," the sheets being simply encased in boards. If a book is of an ephemeral character the edges may be cut at once; otherwise they should be left untouched, or merely trimmed on the fore-edge and foot.

The proper and full title should be lettered on the back of the volume, together with the author's name, and the date at foot. This rule saves unnecessary handling when a particular book is sought. This should be done even in a thin volume, because the lettering may be along the back. The better way is to have it lettered from top to foot, so that if the volume is placed face upwards on the shelf this back lettering is still readable. On the other hand, some prefer it to read from foot to head.

Wire sewing should never be allowed : it tears the paper, and, frequently rusting, stains the leaves. These faults, and the excessive reduction of margins, are never forgiven by a book-lover. Cotton or silk thread should only be used.

Where a large number of copies has been printed off, a portion only should be bound—the publishers should be consulted as to this—for there may not be a demand at first for the whole.

The term " bound " is more strictly applied to leather work, or at least when there is some leather used in the binding—each copy being separately bound together "in-boarded" and not simply cased. There are several degrees of binding in this form : " Quarter bound," having a leather back with cloth or paper sides : this, with gilt top and cloth sides, is called " Roxburghe." "Half bound " has leather back and corners, and cloth or paper sides. "Full bound," when wholly encased in leather.

If the volume has been printed on hand-made paper, the heads only should be cut and gilt, to prevent dirt getting between the leaves. If the fore-edge or tails are very uneven they should be very lightly trimmed, just sufficient to make them tidy. It is a good rule, when taking such a book from its shelf, and before opening it, to blow the dust gently off the top. This accumulation of dust can only be avoided by the use of air-tight book-cases.

Vellum and parchment are both largely used in the binding of books. They are durable, but quickly soiled.

Expensive plates should only be stitched or pasted on to guards of strong paper or linen, as used in atlases, and then sewn in with the different sections of the work.

Rules have been laid down for the binding of works on certain subjects, to form a library, so that each subject may be in a different and appropriate colour; but this must be left to the taste of the owner. However, some thought should be given to the nature of the work. Historical books should bear a distinct shade from those, say, on theology; dictionaries and other works of reference a different hue from poetry, and so forth.

If the reader of this volume is interested in full bindings, he is referred to the different reports of the Committee on leather for bookbindings, formed by the Society of Arts, and issued by that society in 1901. He will there find much useful information and valuable hints as to the care of bound books.

CHAPTER VIII

PUBLISHING

THE Book being now printed and bound—how can it be issued to the public ?

The first step is to find a suitable publisher. Many authors, even those experienced in the ways of books, employ a literary agent for this work, as they not only are able to suggest the most appropriate publisher for a book dealing with any particular subject—for some publishers make a speciality of certain subjects—but also are able afterwards to help the author in technical matters with which he may not be fully conversant. The Incorporated Society of Authors also helps with advice and offers assistance in suggesting a publisher.

As every publisher deals with his clients in a slightly different way, it would be useless to go into details. The best advice that can be given is to approach only those who are well known.

The author, or his agent, having decided upon a publisher, the first thing is to submit the MS. to him.

Never *call* on a publisher with a MS., for no verbal explanation is ever necessary. If it cannot and does not explain itself to him, much less will it explain itself to the public.

When sending the copy, make it up into a *flat* parcel, so that there may be no folds in the paper, which are a great hindrance to reading, and never roll it into a cylindrical form, for this is even more inconvenient than folding.

After the MS. has been sent, the author must not expect a reply by return, for although in large firms competent and special readers are retained to report on proposed works, the number of these submitted is so large that time must necessarily be taken when dealing with them. In some firms from twelve to twenty different manuscripts are received for consideration *per day!* and it is currently said that only ten per cent. of all the books written are ever published.

All arrangements should be in writing, and any agreement entered into should be thoroughly understood.

Books are by no means always commercial successes, and a publisher often runs a risk in taking a work by an unknown writer; his terms are therefore adjusted with a view to protecting himself; and the author too, if he shares the cost of production.

A rough rule for settling the price at which most books may be sold is to treble the cost. Supposing the entire cost—printing, binding, etc. —of an edition of 1,000 to be £100, treble it equals £300, and this sum divided by 1,000=6s.

the price at which each copy may be sold ; the second third being absorbed by trade discounts ; and the final third profits to author and publisher respectively.   This calculation is based on ordinary books, and not those sold at net prices.

All methods of agreement between author and publisher come under one of the following five heads :

(1)   Sale outright.
(2)   Limited sale.
(3)   Profit-sharing.
(4)   Royalty.
(5)   Commission.

(1) Sale outright to the publisher is sometimes the best for the author, as he gets one cheque for all his work ; saves trouble as far as possible ; and avoids all dispute.

The only difficulty of course here is to decide upon a " fair price."

Under (2), limited sale, the author may sell his rights for a limited time, or a limited number of copies.   This is not a common form of agreement.

(3) Profit-sharing, including in this term not only half, but all other proportions of profit, such as a quarter and three-quarters, is very simple, and should be satisfactory to the author.   It has, however, almost died out, as the author is not in a position to know what the whole real profits amount to ; still less therefore the amount of his own fraction.   Should this system be adopted, cost

of production should not be included without investigation ; American, colonial, serial, or translation rights should not be relinquished without a consideration ; future work must not be promised.

The royalty system (4) is perhaps the most popular. In this method the publisher produces the book at his own cost and pays the author a fixed royalty on the published price of every copy :

A. From the beginning;

B. After a certain number have been sold ;

C. After the sales have covered the cost of production.

The first (A) is to be preferred. If the ordinary 6s. novel is published on these terms with a $12\frac{1}{2}$ or 15 per cent. royalty on the published price (6s.), by the time an edition of a thousand or more has been disposed of, the profits of author and publisher will be practically the same. They will, in fact, each have "half-profits."

In publishing on commission (5), the author pays the whole cost of production, and a percentage— usually ten—to the publisher for his services as agent. This is a very large branch of the trade : many works can indeed only be published on these terms, such as some on philosophy, science, technology, poetry, and at least three-quarters of modern fiction !

If the author be a business man and does not object to the trouble this system involves—for he should superintend all the printing and binding,

F

and merely send the finished copies to the publisher for sale—he will probably make more by his book if it is successful than by any other system. But then so many authors will not systematically, and twice a year, work at what they call "accounts," which must here be done to obtain satisfactory results. Care should be taken to obtain a fair cost of production, and to keep control of the advertisements, and also the sale price of the book.

A variation of the commission system is publishing by "subscription." Subscribers are those who promise to take a copy at a certain price, and when a sufficient number have agreed, and thus practically guaranteed the author against loss, the book is put in hand and published. Expensive works—county histories and art volumes—are thus frequently produced when otherwise there would be no chance of their publication.

Before any prospectus is issued it is very necessary that the author or editor should obtain from a responsible printer a complete estimate of the approximate cost of the volume in all respects —not forgetting to allow some margin for the inevitable extras, in the nature of small type and corrections, that spring up in the course of seeing the work through the press.

To secure the subscription price in advance, a smaller one may be asked for at first, which will be raised on issue. If the printer is accustomed to this class of work, he can frequently impart useful information and advice.

Some such form as the accompanying is generally used for soliciting subscriptions :

M ....

        Please enter my name as a subscriber for ....

cop .... *of the work entitled* ....

by .... *for which I undertake*

to pay .... *on delivery* [*or enclose*].

        Name ....

        Address ....

        ....

Date ....

This scheme may be modified if necessary. Should there be two editions, large and small paper, this should be stated, and room for choice allowed in the order-form.

In all editions limited to a certain number of copies, a certificate should be printed in each volume stating :

** *This is to certify that only*   *copies of this edition have been printed, all of which are numbered* [*and signed*].

    No.

        Signed ....

If there are two editions to be printed, they may both be expressed in the certificate, but the numbers of the two sizes can either be distinct and each start at No. 1, or, if preferred, be continuous.

The large paper or special copies should come first.

Ordinary books are frequently issued having a limited large paper edition struck off at the same time. These are generally subscribed for in the manner just mentioned.

Directly a work is ready to be issued by the publisher, it is customary to send certain copies for review to various newspapers and journals. The character of the work must be considered before sending them out broadcast, or perhaps they may be sent where no notice will be taken of them. The publisher generally knows where to place these copies, but the author should mention any particular papers to which he desires them to be sent. Good notices of a work materially add to its success.

Advertising a work is another very important matter. In arranging for this with a publisher, supposing it is a commission book, the author should name some limit. If the advertisement can be included with other books in a general way, the expense is not so great; but the announcement of a work singly is expensive.

Insurance, too, must not be overlooked if the book is a commission one, and the author may either insure the stock himself, or give instructions that it should be covered.

Presentation or gratis copies are frequently sent out in order to give the book a fillip, the copies generally allotted to the writer as "author's copies" probably being distributed amongst his more immediate friends.

All criticisms on the book are filed by the publisher, and use may be made of the best of them should it be necessary to send out a prospectus. Some extracts from these opinions of the press may be included in any future advertisement of the volume.

Most publishers, and sometimes authors too, subscribe to some press-cutting agency, but it is very advisable to see that a competent firm is employed.

CHAPTER IX

COPYRIGHT

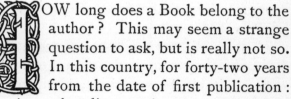OW long does a Book belong to the author ? This may seem a strange question to ask, but is really not so. In this country, for forty-two years from the date of first publication : or while the author lives and seven years afterwards, whichever term be the longer.

The term of copyright for a posthumous work is forty-two years from the date of first publication; the possessor of the MS. being the owner of the copyright.

By Act of Parliament one copy of the *best* edition of each work, and of each subsequent edition, must be despatched at once to the British Museum, London ; and four copies may be sent to Stationers' Hall for the public libraries at Oxford, Cambridge, Dublin, and Edinburgh. In the event of the work running to more than one edition, it is only necessary to send the first issue to the last four libraries, providing no additions have been made to the work. The Librarian of the British Museum and the Officer of the Stationers' Company give receipts for all copies delivered to them. If by chance any of these copies for the libraries are delayed or overlooked, a demand is soon made, generally through the appointed agent, and must be complied with.

Privately-printed books for presentation and not sold in the ordinary way, nor advertised, are supposed to be exempt from the demands of the libraries, though a copy is often sent voluntarily to the British Museum.

With regard to Registration at Stationers' Hall, this stands in a somewhat peculiar position. For some time after printing was first introduced into this country, copyrights were almost exclusively the property of members of the Stationers' Company, and the governing body, to prevent disputes, made a rule requiring all their members to enter their "copies" in a register which was kept at Stationers' Hall. This register, commenced in the fourteenth century, has been continued to the present time, at first under a private ordinance of the company, subsequently continued in accordance with the decrees of the Star Chamber, and afterwards in accordance with the provisions of divers Acts of Parliament. Under the present Copyright Act, which was passed in 1842, registration is not a compulsory matter, but should anyone desire to bring an action for infringement of his copyright he must first register his book and the exact date of first publication. A five-shilling fee is payable to the Registering Officer when the application is made, and the title of the Book is then entered on the Register.

It is essential that the precise terms of the Statute be complied with, and upon application to " The Registrar, Stationers' Hall, London," he will forward full printed instructions, the following extract from which will be found useful :

Mode of Registration.—A proprietor of copyright desiring to register at Stationers' Hall must lodge there a demand signed by him and witnessed, in the form printed on the back thereof, *together with a* fee of 5*s.* for each entry.

Special care should be taken that the full and proper title of the book, and the correct *day, month, and year of first publication* are entered, as any error or omission may invalidate the entry.

A book cannot be registered *before it is published.*

A proprietor of the copyright in an encyclopædia, review, magazine, periodical work, or other work published in a series of books or parts, will be entitled to all the benefits of registration upon his registering the first volume, number, or part.

Assignments.—Registered copyrights, or any share or shares thereof, may be assigned, without payment of any stamp duty, by the registered proprietor lodging, at Stationers' Hall, an entry signed by him in the form prescribed by the Statute, together with a fee of 5*s.* Forms of Assignment can be obtained at Stationers' Hall.

Certified Copies of entries are supplied on payment of a fee of 5*s.* each, and such copies are *primâ facie* proof of the matters alleged therein.

Searches.—A printed Lexicographical Index of all Literary Works registered between 1842 and 1897 is now provided for the use of persons desirous of searching the Book Register. The statutory fee for each entry searched for is 1*s.*

British Possessions.—Books first published in any British Possession which does not provide for registration should be registered at Stationers' Hall.

International Copyright.—Under the provisions of the Berne Convention, books copyright in Great Britain are protected in the following countries :—Belgium, France, Germany, Italy, Spain, Switzerland, Tunis, Hayti, Luxembourg, Monaco, Montenegro, and Norway.

United States, &c.—To secure copyright in Great Britain of works intended to be published in America and other foreign countries (except the Kingdoms and States represented in the Austrian Reichsrath) which have not adopted the provisions of the Berne Convention, simultaneous publication in both countries is essential, and the work should be registered at Stationers' Hall, and one copy delivered to the British Museum, and four copies lodged at Stationers' Hall for the Public Libraries. The name of the *British* publisher and place of publication must in all cases be entered in the register.

Foreign Reprints.—Proprietors of books first composed, or written, or printed in the United Kingdom, desiring to prevent the importation of foreign reprints, must give notice in writing to the Commissioners of Customs, accompanied by a statutory declaration that the copyright subsists, and when it will expire. Registration at Stationers' Hall is also necessary before duties can be levied for the benefit of the proprietor of copyright on foreign reprints of British copyright works imported into the Bahamas, Barbados, Bermuda, British Guiana, Cape of Good Hope, Grenada, Jamaica, Natal, Nova Scotia, Newfoundland, Prince Edward Island, St. Christopher, St. Lucia, and St. Vincent.

It should be noted that one of the conditions of copyright being granted in the United States is that a work must be printed from type actually set up in America.

As before said, in the case of omission to register a work in this country, and there is a presumed infringement of any work, priority of publication is generally accepted as evidence, providing the demands of the five public libraries have been met.

Although the Act of Parliament does not require a book to be registered at Stationers' Hall immediately after publication, it is a wise and prudent course to adopt, as, if delayed, difficulties often arise in supplying the needful particulars in after years; and when once registered, transfers of the copyright are exempt from stamp duty, whether the consideration for the transfer be in tens or hundreds or thousands of pounds.

A SHORT GLOSSARY

OF BIBLIOGRAPHICAL AND TYPOGRAPHICAL TERMS IN
MORE GENERAL USE.

DDENDA (pl.), *Addendum* (s.).—An addi
tion to any work.

Advance sheets (or *copies*).—Sometimes supplied for simultaneous publication, or
preliminary notices.

Ampersand.—A corruption of the words
"*and* per se *and*"—the short sign being & or *&*. .

Antiqua.—A German expression for roman types.

Antique Roman.—A somewhat heavy face of type, a fashion
which the Kelmscott Press books suggested. See specimens
at the end of this volume.

Arabic figures.—Ordinary figures, roman or italic, thus—1 2 3,
etc., as distinct from roman numerals, i, ii, iii, etc.

Art paper.—Coated papers adapted for half-tone block printing
are usually, but inappropriately, so called.

Atlas.—A size of paper, 36 × 26 inches. Folio, 26 × 18;
quarto, 18 × 13; octavo, 13 × 9.

Author's proof.—A proof bearing corrections made by the
author or editor. A. P. is the short expression.

Backs.—The "back" margin of pages—that margin next the
binding.

Bastard title.—A fly- or half-title before the full title of a work.

Black-letter.—A general expression used to indicate 𝔬𝔩𝔡
𝔈𝔫𝔤𝔩𝔦𝔰𝔥, gothic text, or church type.

Bleed.—When a book or pamphlet has been cut down too
much, so as to touch the printed matter, it is said to "bleed."

Blind blocked (or *tooled*).—Simple impressed lettering on book-
covers, not inked or gilt.

Blind P (or *paragraph mark* ¶).—Frequently used in old
printed books.

Blocks.—A general term embracing woodcuts, electros, etc.

Body of the work.—The text or subject-matter of a volume is thus described, to distinguish it from the preliminary, index, appendix, and notes.

Bolts.—The folded or doubled edge of paper at the head and fore-edge.

Bottom notes.—Footnotes are sometimes so called, to distinguish them from sidenotes.

Bourgeois.—Pronounced Burjoice ; a size of type having eight and a half lines to the inch.

Bracket.—A square sign [as distinct from the round sign (or parenthesis. The bracket is sometimes used by the printer to indicate a new paragraph.

Brevier.—Pronounced Bre-veer ; a size of type having nine and a half lines to the inch.

Broadside.—A sheet printed on one side only, such as a poster.

Calendered paper.—Paper very highly rolled or glazed, much used for printing illustrations.

Cancel.—A term used for a new leaf or leaves reprinted in consequence of some error or defect.

Capitals.—Letters thus, CAPITALS. Shortly called " caps."

Caps. and Small Caps.—CAPITALS and SMALL CAPITALS.

Caret.—The sign ∧ used to indicate an insertion in MS. or proofs.

Catchline.—The bottom line of a page, containing the " catch-word " only, which is the first on the next page—now almost obsolete.

Catch-word.—*See* above ; also the first word in an index entry.

Certificate.—A guarantee of a limited number of copies only having been printed of any work, usually placed near the title-page.

Circuit edges.—Books, generally bibles or prayer-books, with the covers projecting and turned over, so as to protect the edges.

Clarendon.—Generally **a bold or fat-faced type** ; the older founts were called " Egyptian."

Clean proof.—One ready to be sent out to the author : not a printer's first proof.

Clean sheets.—Sheets put aside as they are printed off to show the progress of the work.

Cliché.—A stereo or electrotype plate.

Cloth boards.—Books bound in cloth cases.

Cobb paper.—A paper in various shades of colour largely used by binders for the sides of books.

Collotype.—A method of printing from a slightly raised gelatine film produced by photographic means.

Colophon.—An inscription, device, or tailpiece at the end of a book, usually a printer's imprint.

Columbia.—A size of paper, $34\frac{1}{2} \times 23\frac{1}{2}$ inches. Folio, $23\frac{1}{2} \times 17\frac{1}{4}$; quarto, $17\frac{1}{4} \times 11\frac{3}{4}$; octavo, $11\frac{1}{4} \times 8\frac{7}{8}$.

Copperplate.—A term applied generally to those methods of illustration by intaglio, as distinct from blocks in relief.

Copy.—Manuscript for the printer.

Corrigenda (pl.), *Corrigendum* (s.).—A table containing corrections at the end or commencement of a work.

Cropped.—A book with pages cut down too much is said to be "cropped."

Crown.—A sheet measuring 20×15 inches. Folio, 15×10; quarto, $10 \times 7\frac{1}{2}$; octavo, $7\frac{1}{2} \times 5$.

Cursive.—The German expression for *italic* types.

Cut edges.—A book with pages machine-cut on the three edges.

Cut-in notes.—Those inserted within the text at the side, and not in the margin.

Dead reprint.—An absolute facsimile reprint, line for line and page for page.

Decimo-sexto.—The same as sixteenmo, *q.v.*

Deckle.—The raw, rough edge of hand-made paper.

Dele (or *delete*).—To expunge, cancel, delete, or omit, indicated thus δ.

Demy.—A size of printing paper, $22\frac{1}{2} \times 17\frac{1}{2}$ inches. Folio, $17\frac{1}{2} \times 11\frac{1}{4}$; quarto, $11\frac{1}{4} \times 8\frac{3}{4}$; octavo, $8\frac{3}{4} \times 5\frac{5}{8}$.

Diamond.—A size of type having seventeen lines to the inch.

Double Crown.—A sheet measuring 30×20 inches; double the size of Crown, which see.

Double foolscap.—A size of printing paper, 27×17 inches; double the size of Foolscap, which see.

Double Pica.—A size of type having three and a half lines to the inch.

Double pott.—A size of paper, 25 × 15½ inches; double the size of Pott, which see.

Dropped heads.—First pages of chapters, printed lower down the page than ordinarily.

Dummy copy.—One generally made of blank leaves, to represent the bulk of a work.

Duodecimo.—Commonly called twelvemo. A book having twelve leaves to the sheet. Written 12mo.

Dutch papers.—Van Gelder's hand-made papers, made in Holland.

Edition de luxe.—An elaborate, costly and limited edition on large paper.

Egyptian.—*See* "Clarendon."

Eighteenmo.—A book having eighteen leaves to the sheet, written shortly 18mo. Bibliographically termed "octodecimo."

Electrotyping.—A means of duplicating woodcuts, etc., by an electro deposit of copper, which is afterwards backed up by a kind of type metal.

End leaves (or *papers*).—The blank flyleaves at each end of a book.

English.—A size of type having five and a quarter lines to the inch.

Errata (pl.), *Erratum* (s.).—A list of errors, not necessarily printers' errors.

Even pages.—The left-hand or verso pages of a book.

Fine paper edition.—The best edition of a book; sometimes expressed by the letters F. P.

Finishing.—The lettering or tooling on a book-cover.

Flat pull (or *impression*).—A simple proof without under- or over-laying.

Flexible.—A style of binding which allows the book to open quite flat.

Flyleaf.—A blank leaf at each end of a book.

Fly-title.—The half-title in front of the general title, or the one dividing sections of a work.

Folio.—A sheet of paper folded in two leaves only.

Foolscap.—A sheet measuring $17 \times 13\frac{1}{2}$ inches. Folio, $13\frac{1}{2} \times 8\frac{1}{2}$; quarto, $8\frac{1}{2} \times 6\frac{3}{4}$; octavo, $6\frac{3}{4} \times 4\frac{1}{4}$.

Fore-edge.—The edge of a book opposite the binding.

Format.—The bibliographical expression for the size and shape of a book.

Forme.—A printer's term for a number of type-pages imposed in an iron frame called a "chase."

Forwarding.—The different stages in binding between the sewing and finishing of a book, *i.e.*, lettering the title, colouring or gilding the edges, etc.

Fount.—Pronounced font. The whole number of letters, etc., in one complete set of type.

Foxed.—Paper or books which are stained or mouldy.

F. P.—The short abbreviation for fine paper copies of a work.

Fractur.—The German expression for their text or black-letter characters.

Frontispiece.—The picture or plate facing the title-page of a book.

Full bound.—A book wholly bound in leather.

Full point.—The printers' expression for a full stop.

Galley proofs.—Those supplied in slips about two feet long, before the matter is made up into pages.

Gilt tops.—Books with the top edges cut and gilt, to prevent them being soiled by the dust which collects there.

Gratis copies.—Those copies not sold, but sent out for presentation, review, etc.

Great Primer.—A size of type having four and a quarter lines to the inch.

Guarded.—Books are said to be "guarded" when the plates are mounted or sewn on guards (as maps are), instead of being stitched or pasted in the ordinary way.

Hair leads.—Very thin leads for spacing out printed matter. Frequently they measure sixteen to a pica, or ninety-six to an inch.

Hair space.—The thinnest space made for placing between words.

Half bound.—Books bound with leather back and corners, and cloth or paper sides.

Half-title.—The short title in front of the full title.

Half-tone blocks.—Photographic relief printing blocks, produced with the aid of a screen, which breaks the picture up into various tones.

Heads.—The margin at the top of the page.

Imperfections.—Sheets required by a binder to complete books imperfect through bad gathering, collating, or spoiled sheets.

Imperial.—A size of printing paper, 30 × 22 inches. Folio, 22 × 15; quarto, 15 × 11; octavo, 11 × 7½.

Imposition.—A term applied generally to the laying-down of the pages in certain positions, to form, when printed, quartos, octavos, etc.

Imprint.—The printer's name and address in a book, which is necessary by Act of Parliament.

Indent.—To set back any line or lines, as in the commencement of a paragraph.

In quires.—Unbound books in sheets.

In slip.—Galley-proofs printed before making-up into pages.

In the press.—A work in the course of being printed is thus announced.

India paper.—A fine paper used for engraver's proofs. It is generally imported from China, though called " India."

India rubbered.—Books with plates are sometimes coated at the back with a solution of india rubber to save stitching or expense of guarding : when open the book will lie perfectly flat.

Inferior figures and letters.—Made to range at the bottom of a letter, thus— 1 2 3 a e i o u

Initial letters.—Large block or floriated letters used at the commencement of a chapter or work.

Inset.—A sheet, or part of one, placed inside another sheet to complete sequence of pagination.

Intaglio.—A term used for printing from an incised copperplate; the reverse of ordinary or " relief " printing.

Italic.—The *sloping characters*, distinct from roman types, invented by *Aldus Manutius, the Venetian printer.*

Japanese paper.—Hand-made paper with a vellum surface manu-factured in Japan.

Justification.—The exact spacing out to a given measure in type-setting.

Keep standing.—An order not to distribute the type, pending possible reprinting.

Laid paper.—Those papers that show, when held up to the light, parallel waterlines, at intervals of an inch or so.

Large paper.—The best copies of a work with large margins, etc. ; also termed *édition de luxe.* Sometimes expressed by the initials L. P.

Leaded matter.—Lines of type separated by leads, or narrow strips of metal.

Leatherette or *Leatheroid.*—An imitation of leather, usually made of embossed paper.

Leaves.—Must not be confused with pages, because the leaf being printed on both sides is equal to two pages.

Letter paper.—A term for quarto paper : note paper being octavo.

Letterpress.—Matter printed from type as distinct from litho-graphic or plate printing.

Ligatures—Tied letters cast on one body, thus, fi ff fl ffi ffl & sh ft sk, etc.

Line process block.—A direct photographic relief printing block, suitable for ordinary work in line, or drawings in "black and white."

Lining papers.—Papers used by bookbinders for pasting down on and inside the covers.

Literals (or *letterals*).—Single errors by the printer in setting up type—a first proof is usually well sprinkled with such before it is submitted to the author.

Lithography.—Printing from the surface of a smooth but porous stone, invented by Aloys Senefelder over one hundred years ago.

LL.—The abbreviation for "leaves" in a book.

Long Primer.—A size of type having seven and a half lines to the inch.

Lower-case letters.—The small letters, a, b, c, d, e, f, g, etc., not capitals.

Mackle.—A printed sheet with a slurred appearance, owing to some mechanical defect in the impression.

Make-up.—To measure off matter into pages.

Marbled edges.—When the cut edges of books represent marble.

Margin.—The blank paper surrounding a page of print.

Marginalia.—The bibliographical term for marginal notes.

Medium.—A size of printing paper, 24 × 19 inches. Folio, 19 × 12 ; quarto, 12 × 9½ ; octavo, 9½ × 6.

Mezzotint.—An elaborate but effective method of illustration from an intaglio copperplate engraved by hand.

Minion.—A size of type having ten and one-eighth lines to the inch.

Modern face type.—That class of type mostly used in newspaper printing. See specimens at the end of this volume.

Moulds.—The preliminary stage in stereotyping by the paper process. They are also used for plaster work and electro-typing.

Movable.—A general term applied to type to distinguish it from stereotype, etc.

N. D.—An abbreviation denoting "no date" on a book.

Nonpareil.—A size of type having twelve lines to the inch.

Note papers.—Papers octavo in shape, but of various sizes ; letter papers being quarto shape, and also of various sizes.

N. P.—An abbreviation for new paragraph, either in MS. or in corrected proof.

Octavo.—Shortly written 8vo. A book having eight leaves to the sheet.

Octodecimo.—Written shortly 18mo. A book having eighteen leaves to the sheet.

Odd pages.—The right-hand or recto pages of a book.

Off-cut.—That part of the sheet which has to be cut off in order that the sheet may be folded correctly, as in a "twelvemo."

Off-set.—The set-off of ink from one sheet to another, a result of bad ink or insufficient drying.

Old English.—Founts of type of 𝔟𝔩𝔞𝔠𝔨-𝔩𝔢𝔱𝔱𝔢𝔯 character. Sometimes expressed by O. E.

Old face type.—That class of type designed and cut by William Caslon in the early part of the eighteenth century. See specimens at the end of this volume.

Old style type.—Generally used for the best class of bookwork, and known as the "revived old style." It was first designed and cut by Messrs. Miller and Richard about the middle of the nineteenth century. See specimens at the end of this volume.

O. P.—An abbreviation for "out of print."

Overcast.—A particular kind of book-sewing which allows the book when open to lie flat.

Overlays.—The making-ready of an illustration by cutting out varied thicknesses of paper to give light and shade to the design by altering pressure upon the block.

Overplus.—The "plus" or "over" copies of a definite number in printing.

P.—An abbreviation for the word "page." The plural is "pp."

Page.—This must not be confused with a leaf or leaves. Each leaf, being printed on both sides, is equal to two pages.

Paragon.—A size of type having three and three-quarter lines to the inch.

Paste-downs.—The blank flyleaves, sometimes coloured, at each end of a book, which are pasted down on the covers.

Pearl.—A size of type having fifteen lines to the inch.

Photogravure.—A mechanical intaglio process superseding the hand-engraved copperplate.

Pica.—A size of type having six lines to the inch.

Pointing.—The general term used by printers for punctuation. "Stiff pointing" is matter well peppered with commas and other punctuation marks.

Points.—All marks of punctuation.

Post.—A size of printing paper, 20×16 inches.

Pott.—A sheet measuring $15\frac{1}{2} \times 12\frac{1}{2}$ inches. Folio, $12\frac{1}{2} \times 7\frac{3}{4}$; quarto, $7\frac{3}{4} \times 6\frac{1}{4}$; octavo, $6\frac{1}{4} \times 3\frac{7}{8}$.

Preliminary.—Any matter coming before the main body of a work—title, preface, contents, etc.

Press proof.—The final proof marked by the author or editor "press."

Prima.—In reading a work sheet by sheet the first word of the ensuing signature is marked by the reader as the "prima."

Process blocks.—Illustrations produced by photography, and mechanical or chemical processes.

Proof.—A trial print from type, plates, or blocks.

Proof.—A bookbinder's term for some rough edges left on a trimmed book, to show that it has not been cut down excessively.

Publisher's binding.—Cloth binding.

Quad papers.—Those papers made in large size, such as quad crown, 30 × 40 in.—four times the size of crown, 20 × 15 in.

Quadrat.—Blank pieces of metal used by the printer to fill up short lines.

Quarter bound.—Books bound with the back only of leather.

Quarto.—Written shortly 4to. A book having four leaves to the sheet.

Quaternions.—Printed sheets folded and insetted in sections of four.

Query.—A mark (?) made by the corrector of the press to call attention to a possible error.

Quinternions.—Printed sheets folded and insetted in sections of five.

Quire.—Twenty-four sheets of paper.

Quires.—Unbound books in sheets are said to be in quires.

Ream.—Paper in parcels or bundles of a certain size, a printer's ream being 516 sheets. Hand-made and drawing papers may contain 472, 480, or 500 sheets.

Recto.—The right-hand pages of any book.

Register.—The adjustment of print on one side of a leaf to that on the other.

Relief printing.—Letterpress and block printing, as distinct from lithography or plate printing.

Removes.—The difference between one size of type and another.

Retree.—The rejected or slightly damaged paper of different reams, marked × ×. Distinct from outsides or "broken," marked × × ×

Revise.—A proof bearing author's corrections, which has to be submitted again before being sent to press.

Revived old style type.—*See* "Old style type."

Roman.—The class of type (such as this fount) distinguished from *italic* or fancy types. It is called "antiqua" by the Germans.

Roman numerals.—i, ii, iii, iv, etc. The pagination of the preliminary matter of a volume is generally thus expressed.

Roxburghe binding.—A quarter-bound book with top edge gilt.

Royal. A size of printing paper, 25×20 inches. Folio, $20 \times 12\frac{1}{2}$; quarto, $12\frac{1}{2} \times 10$; octavo, $10 \times 6\frac{1}{4}$.

RP.—An abbreviation for "reprint."

Rubricated.—Printed in red ink.

Ruby.—A size of type having fourteen lines to the inch.

Runners.—Figures or letters placed down the side margin of a page to indicate the position of any given line.

Script.—Type similar in character to handwriting.

Serif.—The fine lines on the top and bottom of a letter, as in H. A sanserif is **H**.

Set off.—When the ink transfers from one sheet to another.

Sextodecimo.—A bibliographical term for 16mo.

Shoulder notes.—Marginal notes placed at the top corner of the page.

Sidenotes.—Notes in the side margin, distinct from "footnotes."

Signature.—The letter or figure at the foot of the first page of a sheet, used to identify any particular sheet.

Sixteenmo.—Written shortly, 16mo. A book having sixteen leaves to the sheet, usually about $4\frac{1}{2} \times 7$ inches.

Size copy.—A thickness or dummy copy of blank paper to show a specimen of size and binding.

Slips.—Matter pulled as proofs in long slips, and not made up into pages.

Small capitals.—The SMALLER CAPITALS, as distinct from full CAPITALS, indicated in MS. by underlining with two strokes.

Small paper.—The ordinary copies of a work. Sometimes expressed by the initials S. P.

Small Pica.—A size of type having seven lines to the inch.

Sprinkled edges.—Cut edges of books finely sprinkled with colour.

Stabbed.—A cheap form of stitching by piercing or stabbing, used mostly for pamphlet work.

Standing matter.—When a volume has been printed off and kept standing in type by order.

Start.—Leaves of books are said to "start" when they are loose through defective sewing.

Stereotypes.—Plates cast in metal from movable types, either by "plaster" or "paper" processes.

Stet.—A Latin word written in the margin to cancel any alteration, dots being placed underneath the alteration itself . . . .

Style of the house.—Methods of setting titles, quotations, spellings, etc., peculiar to each printing office.

Sub-title.—The bastard- or half-title placed before the general title. Same as "fly-title."

Super-calendered paper.—Highly rolled paper for dry printing.

Superior letters and figures.—Small letters cast at the top of type, and used for references or abbreviations, M^r, N^o, [1] [2] [3].

Super royal.—A size of printing paper, $27\frac{1}{2} \times 20\frac{1}{2}$ inches. Folio, $20\frac{1}{2} \times 13\frac{3}{4}$; quarto, $13\frac{3}{4} \times 10\frac{1}{4}$; octavo, $10\frac{1}{4} \times 6\frac{7}{8}$.

Swash letters.—Seventeenth-century italic capitals with tails and flourishes, thus—*A B D M N* etc.

Tails.—The bottom or tail-end of a page.

Ternions.—A bibliographical expression for three sheets folded together in folio.

Thick leads.—Strips of metal one twenty-fourth of an inch in thickness, used for separating lines of type.

Thickness copy.—A thickness or dummy copy of blank paper to show a specimen of size and binding.

Thin leads.—Strips of metal one forty-eighth of an inch in thickness, used for separating lines of type.

Thirty-twomo.—Written shortly 32mo. A book having thirty-two leaves to the sheet.

Three-colour process.—The method of printing any coloured picture by the use of the three primary colours superimposed on each other—the blocks being automatically dissected for the purpose in photographing.

Transpose.—Letters or words to be re-arranged as indicated on a proof. Written shortly "trs."

Trigesimo-secundo.—The bibliographical term for "thirty-twomo."

Trimmed edges.—Edges of books cut or trimmed sufficiently to make them tidy without opening head-folds or bolts.

Turned commas.—These are used at each end of an extract or quoted matter. Sometimes called "inverted commas" or "quotation marks."

Twelvemo.—Written shortly 12mo. A book having twelve leaves to the sheet. Also called "duodecimo."

Twenty-fourmo.—Written shortly 24mo. A book having twenty-four leaves to the sheet. Bibliographically termed "vigesimo-quarto."

Two-line letters.—Plain initial letters occupying two lines in depth, used at the commencement of a chapter or work.

Typography.—The art or style of printing from movable letters.

Uncut edges.—Leaves uncut by machinery, not necessarily "unopened" by hand.

Unopened edges.—Applied to books the edges of which have not been opened.

Verso.—The reverse or back of a leaf; the left-hand page of a book; the reverse or opposite of "recto."

Vigesimo-quarto.—The bibliographical term for "twenty-fourmo."

Vignettes.—A class of illustration with the edges undefined and shaded off gradually.

Waste.—Surplus odd sheets of a book beyond the plus copies.

Watermark.—The wire-mark of any particular design woven in a sheet of paper.

White.—The space between any lines or words of type.

White edges.—Edges of books machine-cut, not coloured or gilt.

White out.—To space or "branch out" any composed matter, such as in advertisements.

White paper.—Unprinted paper, whether white or tinted.

Whole-bound.—Books bound entirely in leather, of any kind.

Wire-mark.—Those "laid" marks in paper visible when the sheet is held up to the light.

Woodcuts.—Pictures cut by a knife on wood with the grain, not on the end grain as in modern wood-engraving.

Wood-engraving.—The modern form of illustration on wood, that is, engraved on the end grain of the wood, not cut with the grain.

Wrong fount.—Letters mixed with, but not belonging to, the same fount.   W. F. is the short form.

Xylography.—The cutting and printing of old block-books.

Zincography.—The art of producing engravings on zinc by a chemical process.

SPECIMENS OF TYPES

I N giving these specimens of book-founts, and other examples of simple display types suitable for titles, etc., I have introduced a new feature, which I venture to think will be appreciated by both Authors and Publishers. I have taken a standard writer—Ruskin, in "Sesame and Lilies"—and repeated the same passage in every panel, in order that the comparisons may hold good in each case. These panels have been arranged, as far as possible, 2 inches deep, and are set $3\frac{1}{2}$ inches wide in all cases. Thus $2 \times 3\frac{1}{2} = 7$. If the total number of words quoted at the end of each specimen is divided by seven, the average contained in a square inch in any one size of type, leaded or solid, is arrived at by a very simple process. It will be observed that there is a difference between the several classes of types shown, and it will therefore be necessary to select the particular series required, in order to obtain the approximate number of words in a square inch. This can be verified by a reference to the table on page 92.

INDEX OF TYPES

ANALYSIS OF TYPES

CLASS.	AVERAGE WORDS IN A SQUARE INCH.		
OLD FACE.	*Thick leaded.*	*Thin leaded.*	*Solid.*
GREAT PRIMER . . .	7	8	9
ENGLISH	11	12	14
PICA	14	15	16
SMALL PICA	17	19	23
LONG PRIMER	21	23	27
BOURGEOIS	25	29	34
BREVIER	31	35	39
NONPAREIL	44	52	66
OLD STYLE.			
GREAT PRIMER . . .	7	7	8
ENGLISH	10	11	12
PICA	12	14	15
SMALL PICA	16	19	23
LONG PRIMER	20	24	27
BOURGEOIS	24	28	32
BREVIER	29	33	38
MINION	33	37	44
NONPAREIL	40	47	59
PEARL	55	65	81
ANTIQUE ROMAN.			
GREAT PRIMER . . .	5	6	7
PICA	11	12	14
LONG PRIMER	16	20	23
BREVIER	26	29	33
NONPAREIL	36	42	53
MODERN.			
GREAT PRIMER . . .	6	7	8
ENGLISH	10	11	12
PICA	12	14	15
SMALL PICA	16	19	23
LONG PRIMER	20	24	27
BOURGEOIS	24	27	31
BREVIER	26	31	35
MINION	32	37	43
NONPAREIL	37	44	55
PEARL	52	62	78

N.B.—*Fractions under one-half omitted.   One-half or more reckoned as a unit.*

92

NOTE

IN all cases the Top panel is *thick leaded*;
the Middle panel *thin leaded*; and the
Bottom one set *solid* (without leads).

93 Old Face Great Primer

A book is essentially not a talked thing,
but a written thing; and written, not
with a view of mere communication,
but of permanence.   The book of talk
is printed only because its author cannot
speak to thousands of people at once;
if he could, he would—the volume is

50

A book is essentially not a talked thing,
but a written thing; and written, not
with a view of mere communication,
but of permanence.   The book of talk
is printed only because its author cannot
speak to thousands of people at once;
if he could, he would—the volume is
mere multiplication of his voice.   You

56

A book is essentially not a talked thing,
but a written thing; and written, not
with a view of mere communication,
but of permanence.   The book of talk
is printed only because its author cannot
speak to thousands of people at once;
if he could, he would—the volume is
mere multiplication of his voice.   You
cannot talk to your friend in India; if

64

A book is essentially not a talked thing, but a written thing; and written, not with a view of mere communication, but of permanence. The book of talk is printed only because its author cannot speak to thousands of people at once; if he could, he would—the volume is mere multiplication of his voice. You cannot talk to your friend in India; if you could, you would; you write instead: that is mere conveyance of

76

A book is essentially not a talked thing, but a written thing; and written, not with a view of mere communication, but of permanence. The book of talk is printed only because its author cannot speak to thousands of people at once; if he could, he would—the volume is mere multiplication of his voice. You cannot talk to your friend in India; if you could, you would; you write instead: that is mere conveyance of voice. But a book is written, not to multiply

85

A book is essentially not a talked thing, but a written thing; and written, not with a view of mere communication, but of permanence. The book of talk is printed only because its author cannot speak to thousands of people at once; if he could, he would—the volume is mere multiplication of his voice. You cannot talk to your friend in India; if you could, you would; you write instead: that is mere conveyance of voice. But a book is written, not to multiply the voice merely, not to carry it merely, but to

95

94 Old Face English

95 Old Face Pica

A book is essentially not a talked thing, but a written thing; and written, not with a view of mere communication, but of permanence. The book of talk is printed only because its author cannot speak to thousands of people at once; if he could, he would—the volume is mere multiplication of his voice. You cannot talk to your friend in India; if you could, you would; you write instead : that is mere conveyance of voice. But a book is written, not to multiply the voice merely, not to carry it merely, but to perpetuate

96

A book is essentially not a talked thing, but a written thing; and written, not with a view of mere communication, but of permanence. The book of talk is printed only because its author cannot speak to thousands of people at once; if he could, he would—the volume is mere multiplication of his voice. You cannot talk to your friend in India; if you could, you would; you write instead : that is mere conveyance of voice. But a book is written, not to multiply the voice merely, not to carry it merely, but to perpetuate it. The author has something to say which he per-

106

A book is essentially not a talked thing, but a written thing; and written, not with a view of mere communication, but of permanence. The book of talk is printed only because its author cannot speak to thousands of people at once; if he could, he would—the volume is mere multiplication of his voice. You cannot talk to your friend in India; if you could, you would; you write instead : that is mere conveyance of voice. But a book is written, not to multiply the voice merely, not to carry it merely, but to perpetuate it. The author has something to say which he perceives to be true and useful, or helpfully beautiful.

114

A book is essentially not a talked thing, but a written thing; and written, not with a view of mere communication, but of permanence. The book of talk is printed only because its author cannot speak to thousands of people at once; if he could, he would—the volume is mere multiplication of his voice. You cannot talk to your friend in India; if you could, you would; you write instead: that is mere conveyance of voice. But a book is written, not to multiply the voice merely, not to carry it merely, but to perpetuate it. The author has something to say which he perceives to be true and useful, or helpfully beautiful. So far as he knows, no

120

A book is essentially not a talked thing, but a written thing; and written, not with a view of mere communication, but of permanence. The book of talk is printed only because its author cannot speak to thousands of people at once; if he could, he would—the volume is mere multiplication of his voice. You cannot talk to your friend in India; if you could, you would; you write instead: that is mere conveyance of voice. But a book is written, not to multiply the voice merely, not to carry it merely, but to perpetuate it. The author has something to say which he perceives to be true and useful, or helpfully beautiful. So far as he knows, no one has yet said it; so far as he knows, no one else can say

135

A book is essentially not a talked thing, but a written thing; and written, not with a view of mere communication, but of permanence. The book of talk is printed only because its author cannot speak to thousands of people at once; if he could, he would—the volume is mere multiplication of his voice. You cannot talk to your friend in India; if you could, you would; you write instead: that is mere conveyance of voice. But a book is written, not to multiply the voice merely, not to carry it merely, but to perpetuate it. The author has something to say which he perceives to be true and useful, or helpfully beautiful. So far as he knows, no one has yet said it; so far as he knows, no one else can say it. He is bound to say it, clearly and melodiously if he may; clearly, at all events. In the sum of his life he finds this to

162

96 Old Face Small Pica

97 Old Face Long Primer

A book is essentially not a talked thing, but a written thing; and written, not with a view of mere communication, but of permanence. The book of talk is printed only because its author cannot speak to thousands of people at once; if he could, he would— the volume is mere multiplication of his voice. You cannot talk to your friend in India; if you could, you would; you write instead: that is mere conveyance of voice. But a book is written, not to multiply the voice merely, not to carry it merely, but to perpetuate it. The author has something to say which he perceives to be true and useful, or helpfully beautiful. So far as he knows, no one has yet said it; so far as he knows, no one else can say it. He is bound to say it, clearly and melodiously if he

147

A book is essentially not a talked thing, but a written thing; and written, not with a view of mere communication, but of permanence. The book of talk is printed only because its author cannot speak to thousands of people at once; if he could, he would— the volume is mere multiplication of his voice. You cannot talk to your friend in India; if you could, you would; you write instead: that is mere conveyance of voice. But a book is written, not to multiply the voice merely, not to carry it merely, but to perpetuate it. The author has something to say which he perceives to be true and useful, or helpfully beautiful. So far as he knows, no one has yet said it; so far as he knows, no one else can say it. He is bound to say it, clearly and melodiously if he may; clearly, at all events. In the sum of his life he finds this

161

A book is essentially not a talked thing, but a written thing; and written, not with a view of mere communication, but of permanence. The book of talk is printed only because its author cannot speak to thousands of people at once; if he could, he would— the volume is mere multiplication of his voice. You cannot talk to your friend in India; if you could, you would; you write instead: that is mere conveyance of voice. But a book is written, not to multiply the voice merely, not to carry it merely, but to perpetuate it. The author has something to say which he perceives to be true and useful, or helpfully beautiful. So far as he knows, no one has yet said it; so far as he knows, no one else can say it. He is bound to say it, clearly and melodiously if he may; clearly, at all events. In the sum of his life he finds this to be the thing, or group of things, manifest to him;—this, the piece of true knowledge, or sight, which his share of sunshine and

186

A book is essentially not a talked thing, but a written thing; and written, not with a view of mere communication, but of permanence. The book of talk is printed only because its author cannot speak to thousands of people at once; if he could, he would—the volume is mere multiplication of his voice. You cannot talk to your friend in India; if you could, you would; you write instead : that is mere conveyance of voice. But a book is written, not to multiply the voice merely, not to carry it merely, but to perpetuate it. The author has something to say which he perceives to be true and useful, or helpfully beautiful. So far as he knows, no one has yet said it; so far as he knows, no one else can say it. He is bound to say it, clearly and melodiously if he may; clearly, at all events. In the sum of his life he finds this to be the thing, or group of things, manifest to him;—this, the piece of true knowledge,

178

A book is essentially not a talked thing, but a written thing; and written, not with a view of mere communication, but of permanence. The book of talk is printed only because its author cannot speak to thousands of people at once ; if he could, he would—the volume is mere multiplication of his voice. You cannot talk to your friend in India ; if you could, you would ; you write instead : that is mere conveyance of voice. But a book is written, not to multiply the voice merely, not to carry it merely, but to perpetuate it. The author has something to say which he perceives to be true and useful, or helpfully beautiful. So far as he knows, no one has yet said it ; so far as he knows, no one else can say it. He is bound to say it, clearly and melodiously if he may ; clearly, at all events. In the sum of his life he finds this to be the thing, or group of things, manifest to him ;—this, the piece of true knowledge, or sight, which his share of sunshine and earth has permitted him to seize. He would fain set it down for ever; engrave it on rock, if he

206

A book is essentially not a talked thing, but a written thing; and written, not with a view of mere communication, but of permanence. The book of talk is printed only because its author cannot speak to thousands of people at once ; if he could, he would—the volume is mere multiplication of his voice. You cannot talk to your friend in India ; if you could, you would ; you write instead : that is mere conveyance of voice. But a book is written, not to multiply the voice merely, not to carry it merely, but to perpetuate it. The author has something to say which he perceives to be true and useful, or helpfully beautiful. So far as he knows, no one has yet said it ; so far as he knows, no one else can say it. He is bound to say it, clearly and melodiously if he may ; clearly, at all events. In the sum of his life he finds this to be the thing, or group of things, manifest to him ;—this, the piece of true knowledge, or sight, which his share of sunshine and earth has permitted him to seize. He would fain set it down for ever; engrave it on rock, if he could ; saying, "This is the best of me ; for the rest, I ate, and drank, and slept, loved, and hated, like another ; my life was as the vapour, and

235

98 Old Face Bourgeois

99 Old Face Brevier

A book is essentially not a talked thing, but a written thing; and written, not with a view of mere communication, but of permanence. The book of talk is printed only because its author cannot speak to thousands of people at once; if he could, he would—the volume is mere multiplication of his voice. You cannot talk to your friend in India; if you could, you would; you write instead: that is mere conveyance of voice. But a book is written, not to multiply the voice merely, not to carry it merely, but to perpetuate it. The author has something to say which he perceives to be true and useful, or helpfully beautiful. So far as he knows, no one has yet said it; so far as he knows, no one else can say it. He is bound to say it, clearly and melodiously if he may; clearly, at all events. In the sum of his life he finds this to be the thing, or group of things, manifest to him;—this, the piece of true knowledge, or sight, which his share of sunshine and earth has permitted him to seize. He would fain set it down for ever; engrave it on rock, if he could; saying, "This is the best of me; for

215

A book is essentially not a talked thing, but a written thing; and written, not with a view of mere communication, but of permanence. The book of talk is printed only because its author cannot speak to thousands of people at once; if he could, he would—the volume is mere multiplication of his voice. You cannot talk to your friend in India; if you could, you would; you write instead: that is mere conveyance of voice. But a book is written, not to multiply the voice merely, not to carry it merely, but to perpetuate it. The author has something to say which he perceives to be true and useful, or helpfully beautiful. So far as he knows, no one has yet said it; so far as he knows, no one else can say it. He is bound to say it, clearly and melodiously if he may; clearly, at all events. In the sum of his life he finds this to be the thing, or group of things, manifest to him;—this, the piece of true knowledge, or sight, which his share of sunshine and earth has permitted him to seize. He would fain set it down for ever; engrave it on rock, if he could; saying, "This is the best of me; for the rest, I ate, and drank, and slept, loved, and hated, like another; my life was as the vapour, and is not; but this I saw and knew: this, if anything of mine,

248

A book is essentially not a talked thing, but a written thing; and written, not with a view of mere communication, but of permanence. The book of talk is printed only because its author cannot speak to thousands of people at once; if he could, he would—the volume is mere multiplication of his voice. You cannot talk to your friend in India; if you could, you would; you write instead: that is mere conveyance of voice. But a book is written, not to multiply the voice merely, not to carry it merely, but to perpetuate it. The author has something to say which he perceives to be true and useful, or helpfully beautiful. So far as he knows, no one has yet said it; so far as he knows, no one else can say it. He is bound to say it, clearly and melodiously if he may; clearly, at all events. In the sum of his life he finds this to be the thing, or group of things, manifest to him;—this, the piece of true knowledge, or sight, which his share of sunshine and earth has permitted him to seize. He would fain set it down for ever; engrave it on rock, if he could; saying, "This is the best of me; for the rest, I ate, and drank, and slept, loved, and hated, like another; my life was as the vapour, and is not; but this I saw and knew: this, if anything of mine, is worth your memory." That is his "writing"; it is, in his small human way, and with whatever degree of true inspiration is in him, his inscription, or

276

A book is essentially not a talked thing, but a written thing ; and written, not with a view of mere communication, but of permanence. The book of talk is printed only because its author cannot speak to thousands of people at once ; if he could, he would—the volume is mere multiplication of his voice. You cannot talk to your friend in India ; if you could, you would ; you write instead : that is mere conveyance of voice. But a book is written, not to multiply the voice merely, not to carry it merely, but to perpetuate it. The author has something to say which he perceives to be true and useful, or helpfully beautiful. So far as he knows, no one has yet said it ; so far as he knows, no one else can say it. He is bound to say it, clearly and melodiously if he may ; clearly, at all events. In the sum of his life he finds this to be the thing, or group of things, manifest to him ;—this, the piece of true knowledge, or sight, which his share of sunshine and earth has permitted him to seize. He would fain set it down for ever ; engrave it on rock, if he could ; saying, " This is the best of me ; for the rest, I ate, and drank, and slept, loved, and hated, like another ; my life was as the vapour, and is not ; but this I saw and knew : this, if anything of mine, is worth your memory." That is his " writing " ; it is, in his small human way, and with whatever degree of true inspiration is in him, his inscription, or scripture. That is a " Book." Perhaps you think no books were ever so written ? But, again, I ask you, do you at all believe in honesty, or at all in kindness ? or do you

310

A book is essentially not a talked thing, but a written thing ; and written, not with a view of mere communication, but of permanence. The book of talk is printed only because its author cannot speak to thousands of people at once ; if he could, he would—the volume is mere multiplication of his voice. You cannot talk to your friend in India ; if you could, you would ; you write instead : that is mere conveyance of voice. But a book is written, not to multiply the voice merely, not to carry it merely, but to perpetuate it. The author has something to say which he perceives to be true and useful, or helpfully beautiful. So far as he knows, no one has yet said it ; so far as he knows, no one else can say it. He is bound to say it, clearly and melodiously if he may ; clearly, at all events. In the sum of his life he finds this to be the thing, or group of things, manifest to him ;—this, the piece of true knowledge, or sight, which his share of sunshine and earth has permitted him to seize. He would fain set it down for ever ; engrave it on rock, if he could ; saying, " This is the best of me ; for the rest, I ate, and drank, and slept, loved, and hated, like another ; my life was as the vapour, and is not ; but this I saw and knew : this, if anything of mine, is worth your memory." That is his " writing " ; it is, in his small human way, and with whatever degree of true inspiration is in him, his inscription, or scripture. That is a " Book." Perhaps you think no books were ever so written ? But, again, I ask you, do you at all believe in honesty, or at all in kindness ? or do you think there is never any honesty or benevolence in wise people ? None of us, I hope, are so unhappy as to think that. Well, whatever bit of a wise man's work is honestly and benevolently done, that bit is his book, or his piece of art. It is mixed always with evil fragments—ill-done, redundant,

366

A book is essentially not a talked thing, but a written thing ; and written, not with a view of mere communication, but of permanence. The book of talk is printed only because its author cannot speak to thousands of people at once ; if he could, he would—the volume is mere multiplication of his voice. You cannot talk to your friend in India ; if you could, you would ; you write instead : that is mere conveyance of voice. But a book is written, not to multiply the voice merely, not to carry it merely, but to perpetuate it. The author has something to say which he perceives to be true and useful, or helpfully beautiful. So far as he knows, no one has yet said it ; so far as he knows, no one else can say it. He is bound to say it, clearly and melodiously if he may ; clearly, at all events. In the sum of his life he finds this to be the thing, or group of things, manifest to him ;—this, the piece of true knowledge, or sight, which his share of sunshine and earth has permitted him to seize. He would fain set it down for ever ; engrave it on rock, if he could ; saying, " This is the best of me ; for the rest, I ate, and drank, and slept, loved, and hated, like another ; my life was as the vapour, and is not ; but this I saw and knew : this, if anything of mine, is worth your memory." That is his " writing " ; it is, in his small human way, and with whatever degree of true inspiration is in him, his inscription, or scripture. That is a " Book." Perhaps you think no books were ever so written ? But, again, I ask you, do you at all believe in honesty, or at all in kindness ? or do you think there is never any honesty or benevolence in wise people ? None of us, I hope, are so unhappy as to think that. Well, whatever bit of a wise man's work is honestly and benevolently done, that bit is his book, or his piece of art. It is mixed always with evil fragments—ill-done, redundant, affected work. But if you read rightly, you will easily discover the true bits, and those are the book. Now, books of this kind have been written in all ages by their greatest men,—by great readers, great statesmen, and great thinkers. These are all at your choice ; and Life is short. You have heard as much before ;—yet have you measured and mapped out this short life and its possibilities ? Do you know, if you read this, that you cannot read that—that what you lose to-day you cannot gain to-

459

I

100 Old Face Nonpareil

101 Old Style Great Primer

A book is essentially not a talked thing, but a written thing ; and written, not with a view of mere communication, but of permanence. The book of talk is printed only because its author cannot speak to thousands of people at once ; if he could, he

46

A book is essentially not a talked thing, but a written thing ; and written, not with a view of mere communication, but of permanence. The book of talk is printed only because its author cannot speak to thousands of people at once ; if he could, he would—the volume is mere multipli-

52

A book is essentially not a talked thing, but a written thing ; and written, not with a view of mere communication, but of permanence. The book of talk is printed only because its author cannot speak to thousands of people at once ; if he could, he would—the volume is mere multiplication of his voice. You cannot talk

58

A book is essentially not a talked thing,
but a written thing; and written, not with
a view of mere communication, but of permanence. The book of talk is printed only
because its author cannot speak to thousands of people at once; if he could, he
would—the volume is mere multiplication
of his voice. You cannot talk to your
friend in India; if you could, you would;
68

A book is essentially not a talked thing,
but a written thing; and written, not with
a view of mere communication, but of permanence. The book of talk is printed only
because its author cannot speak to thousands of people at once; if he could, he
would—the volume is mere multiplication
of his voice. You cannot talk to your
friend in India; if you could, you would;
you write instead : that is mere conveyance
75

A book is essentially not a talked thing,
but a written thing; and written, not with
a view of mere communication, but of permanence. The book of talk is printed only
because its author cannot speak to thousands of people at once; if he could, he
would—the volume is mere multiplication
of his voice. You cannot talk to your
friend in India; if you could, you would;
you write instead : that is mere conveyance
of voice. But a book is written, not to
84

102 Old Style English

103 Old Style Pica

A book is essentially not a talked thing, but a written thing; and written, not with a view of mere communication, but of permanence. The book of talk is printed only because its author cannot speak to thousands of people at once; if he could, he would—the volume is mere multiplication of his voice. You cannot talk to your friend in India; if you could, you would; you write instead : that is mere conveyance of voice. But a book is written, not to multiply the voice

A book is essentially not a talked thing, but a written thing; and written, not with a view of mere communication, but of permanence. The book of talk is printed only because its author cannot speak to thousands of people at once; if he could, he would—the volume is mere multiplication of his voice. You cannot talk to your friend in India; if you could, you would; you write instead : that is mere conveyance of voice. But a book is written, not to multiply the voice merely, not to carry it merely, but to perpetuate

A book is essentially not a talked thing, but a written thing; and written, not with a view of mere communication, but of permanence. The book of talk is printed only because its author cannot speak to thousands of people at once; if he could, he would—the volume is mere multiplication of his voice. You cannot talk to your friend in India; if you could, you would; you write instead : that is mere conveyance of voice. But a book is written, not to multiply the voice merely, not to carry it merely, but to perpetuate it. The author has something to say which he

A book is essentially not a talked thing, but a written thing; and written, not with a view of mere communication, but of permanence. The book of talk is printed only because its author cannot speak to thousands of people at once; if he could, he would—the volume is mere multiplication of his voice. You cannot talk to your friend in India; if you could, you would; you write instead : that is mere conveyance of voice. But a book is written, not to multiply the voice merely, not to carry it merely, but to perpetuate it. The author has something to say which he perceives to be true and

A book is essentially not a talked thing, but a written thing; and written, not with a view of mere communication, but of permanence. The book of talk is printed only because its author cannot speak to thousands of people at once; if he could, he would—the volume is mere multiplication of his voice. You cannot talk to your friend in India; if you could, you would; you write instead : that is mere conveyance of voice. But a book is written, not to multiply the voice merely, not to carry it merely, but to perpetuate it. The author has something to say which he perceives to be true and useful, or helpfully beautiful. So far as he knows, no one has yet said it; so far as he knows, no one else can

A book is essentially not a talked thing, but a written thing; and written, not with a view of mere communication, but of permanence. The book of talk is printed only because its author cannot speak to thousands of people at once; if he could, he would—the volume is mere multiplication of his voice. You cannot talk to your friend in India; if you could, you would; you write instead : that is mere conveyance of voice. But a book is written, not to multiply the voice merely, not to carry it merely, but to perpetuate it. The author has something to say which he perceives to be true and useful, or helpfully beautiful. So far as he knows, no one has yet said it; so far as he knows, no one else can say it. He is bound to say it, clearly and melodiously if he may ; clearly, at all events. In the sum of his life

105 Old Style Long Primer

A book is essentially not a talked thing, but a written thing; and written, not with a view of mere communication, but of permanence. The book of talk is printed only because its author cannot speak to thousands of people at once; if he could, he would—the volume is mere multiplication of his voice. You cannot talk to your friend in India; if you could, you would; you write instead: that is mere conveyance of voice. But a book is written, not to multiply the voice merely, not to carry it merely, but to perpetuate it. The author has something to say which he perceives to be true and useful, or helpfully beautiful. So far as he knows, no one has yet said it; so far as he knows, no one else can say it. He is bound to say it,

142

A book is essentially not a talked thing, but a written thing; and written, not with a view of mere communication, but of permanence. The book of talk is printed only because its author cannot speak to thousands of people at once; if he could, he would—the volume is mere multiplication of his voice. You cannot talk to your friend in India; if you could, you would; you write instead: that is mere conveyance of voice. But a book is written, not to multiply the voice merely, not to carry it merely, but to perpetuate it. The author has something to say which he perceives to be true and useful, or helpfully beautiful. So far as he knows, no one has yet said it; so far as he knows, no one else can say it. He is bound to say it, clearly and melodiously if he may; clearly, at all events. In the sum of his life he finds this to be the thing, or group of

168

A book is essentially not a talked thing, but a written thing; and written, not with a view of mere communication, but of permanence. The book of talk is printed only because its author cannot speak to thousands of people at once; if he could, he would—the volume is mere multiplication of his voice. You cannot talk to your friend in India; if you could, you would; you write instead: that is mere conveyance of voice. But a book is written, not to multiply the voice merely, not to carry it merely, but to perpetuate it. The author has something to say which he perceives to be true and useful, or helpfully beautiful. So far as he knows, no one has yet said it; so far as he knows, no one else can say it. He is bound to say it, clearly and melodiously if he may; clearly, at all events. In the sum of his life he finds this to be the thing, or group of things, manifest to him;—this, the piece of true knowledge, or sight, which his share of sunshine and earth has permitted him

190

A book is essentially not a talked thing, but a written thing ; and written, not with a view of mere communication, but of permanence. The book of talk is printed only because its author cannot speak to thousands of people at once ; if he could, he would—the volume is mere multiplication of his voice. You cannot talk to your friend in India ; if you could, you would ; you write instead : that is mere conveyance of voice. But a book is written, not to multiply the voice merely, not to carry it merely, but to perpetuate it. The author has something to say which he perceives to be true and useful, or helpfully beautiful. So far as he knows, no one has yet said it ; so far as he knows, no one else can say it. He is bound to say it, clearly and melodiously if he may ; clearly, at all events. In the sum of his life he finds this to be the thing, or group of things,

169

A book is essentially not a talked thing, but a written thing ; and written, not with a view of mere communication, but of permanence. The book of talk is printed only because its author cannot speak to thousands of people at once ; if he could, he would—the volume is mere multiplication of his voice. You cannot talk to your friend in India ; if you could, you would ; you write instead : that is mere conveyance of voice. But a book is written, not to multiply the voice merely, not to carry it merely, but to perpetuate it. The author has something to say which he perceives to be true and useful, or helpfully beautiful. So far as he knows, no one has yet said it ; so far as he knows, no one else can say it. He is bound to say it, clearly and melodiously if he may ; clearly, at all events. In the sum of his life he finds this to be the thing, or group of things, manifest to him ;—this, the piece of true knowledge, or sight, which his share of sunshine and earth has permitted him to seize. He

193

A book is essentially not a talked thing, but a written thing ; and written, not with a view of mere communication, but of permanence. The book of talk is printed only because its author cannot speak to thousands of people at once ; if he could, he would—the volume is mere multiplication of his voice. You cannot talk to your friend in India ; if you could, you would ; you write instead : that is mere conveyance of voice. But a book is written, not to multiply the voice merely, not to carry it merely, but to perpetuate it. The author has something to say which he perceives to be true and useful, or helpfully beautiful. So far as he knows, no one has yet said it ; so far as he knows, no one else can say it. He is bound to say it, clearly and melodiously if he may ; clearly, at all events. In the sum of his life he finds this to be the thing, or group of things, manifest to him ;—this, the piece of true knowledge, or sight, which his share of sunshine and earth has permitted him to seize. He would fain set it down for ever ; engrave it on rock, if he could ; saying, "This is the best of me ; for the rest, I ate, and drank, and

222

106 Old Style Bourgeois

107 Old Style Brevier

A book is essentially not a talked thing, but a written thing; and written, not with a view of mere communication, but of permanence. The book of talk is printed only because its author cannot speak to thousands of people at once; if he could, he would—the volume is mere multiplication of his voice. You cannot talk to your friend in India; if you could, you would; you write instead : that is mere conveyance of voice. But a book is written, not to multiply the voice merely, not to carry it merely, but to perpetuate it. The author has something to say which he perceives to be true and useful, or helpfully beautiful. So far as he knows, no one has yet said it; so far as he knows, no one else can say it. He is bound to say it, clearly and melodiously if he may; clearly, at all events. In the sum of his life he finds this to be the thing, or group of things, manifest to him;—this, the piece of true knowledge, or sight, which his share of sunshine and earth has permitted him to seize. He would fain set it down for ever; engrave it on

203

A book is essentially not a talked thing, but a written thing; and written, not with a view of mere communication, but of permanence. The book of talk is printed only because its author cannot speak to thousands of people at once; if he could, he would—the volume is mere multiplication of his voice. You cannot talk to your friend in India; if you could, you would; you write instead : that is mere conveyance of voice. But a book is written, not to multiply the voice merely, not to carry it merely, but to perpetuate it. The author has something to say which he perceives to be true and useful, or helpfully beautiful. So far as he knows, no one has yet said it; so far as he knows, no one else can say it. He is bound to say it, clearly and melodiously if he may; clearly, at all events. In the sum of his life he finds this to be the thing, or group of things, manifest to him;—this, the piece of true knowledge, or sight, which his share of sunshine and earth has permitted him to seize. He would fain set it down for ever; engrave it on rock, if he could; saying, "This is the best of me; for the rest, I ate, and drank, and slept, loved, and hated, like another; my life was as the vapour,

234

A book is essentially not a talked thing, but a written thing; and written, not with a view of mere communication, but of permanence. The book of talk is printed only because its author cannot speak to thousands of people at once; if he could, he would—the volume is mere multiplication of his voice. You cannot talk to your friend in India; if you could, you would; you write instead : that is mere conveyance of voice. But a book is written, not to multiply the voice merely, not to carry it merely, but to perpetuate it. The author has something to say which he perceives to be true and useful, or helpfully beautiful. So far as he knows, no one has yet said it; so far as he knows, no one else can say it. He is bound to say it, clearly and melodiously if he may; clearly, at all events. In the sum of his life he finds this to be the thing, or group of things, manifest to him;—this, the piece of true knowledge, or sight, which his share of sunshine and earth has permitted him to seize. He would fain set it down for ever; engrave it on rock, if he could; saying, "This is the best of me; for the rest, I ate, and drank, and slept, loved, and hated, like another; my life was as the vapour, and is not; but this I saw and knew: this, if anything of mine, is worth your memory." That is his "writing"; it is, in his small human way, and

264

A book is essentially not a talked thing, but a written thing; and written, not with a view of mere communication, but of permanence. The book of talk is printed only because its author cannot speak to thousands of people at once; if he could, he would—the volume is mere multiplication of his voice. You cannot talk to your friend in India; if you could, you would; you write instead: that is mere conveyance of voice. But a book is written, not to multiply the voice merely, not to carry it merely, but to perpetuate it. The author has something to say which he perceives to be true and useful, or helpfully beautiful. So far as he knows, no one has yet said it; so far as he knows, no one else can say it. He is bound to say it, clearly and melodiously if he may; clearly, at all events. In the sum of his life he finds this to be the thing, or group of things, manifest to him;—this, the piece of true knowledge, or sight, which his share of sunshine and earth has permitted him to seize. He would fain set it down for ever; engrave it on rock, if he could; saying, "This is the best of me; for the rest, I ate, and drank, and slept, loved, and hated, like another; my life

230

A book is essentially not a talked thing, but a written thing; and written, not with a view of mere communication, but of permanence. The book of talk is printed only because its author cannot speak to thousands of people at once; if he could, he would—the volume is mere multiplication of his voice. You cannot talk to your friend in India; if you could, you would; you write instead: that is mere conveyance of voice. But a book is written, not to multiply the voice merely, not to carry it merely, but to perpetuate it. The author has something to say which he perceives to be true and useful, or helpfully beautiful. So far as he knows, no one has yet said it; so far as he knows, no one else can say it. He is bound to say it, clearly and melodiously if he may; clearly, at all events. In the sum of his life he finds this to be the thing, or group of things, manifest to him;—this, the piece of true knowledge, or sight, which his share of sunshine and earth has permitted him to seize. He would fain set it down for ever; engrave it on rock, if he could; saying, "This is the best of me; for the rest, I ate, and drank, and slept, loved, and hated, like another; my life was as the vapour, and is not; but this I saw and knew: this, if anything of mine, is worth your memory." That is his "writing"; it is, in his small human

262

A book is essentially not a talked thing, but a written thing; and written, not with a view of mere communication, but of permanence. The book of talk is printed only because its author cannot speak to thousands of people at once; if he could, he would—the volume is mere multiplication of his voice. You cannot talk to your friend in India; if you could, you would; you write instead: that is mere conveyance of voice. But a book is written, not to multiply the voice merely, not to carry it merely, but to perpetuate it. The author has something to say which he perceives to be true and useful, or helpfully beautiful. So far as he knows, no one has yet said it; so far as he knows, no one else can say it. He is bound to say it, clearly and melodiously if he may; clearly, at all events. In the sum of his life he finds this to be the thing, or group of things, manifest to him;—this, the piece of true knowledge, or sight, which his share of sunshine and earth has permitted him to seize. He would fain set it down for ever; engrave it on rock, if he could; saying, "This is the best of me; for the rest, I ate, and drank, and slept, loved, and hated, like another; my life was as the vapour, and is not; but this I saw and knew: this, if anything of mine, is worth your memory." That is his "writing"; it is, in his small human way, and with whatever degree of true inspiration is in him, his inscription, or scripture. That is a "Book." Perhaps you think no books were ever so written? But, again, I ask you, do you at all believe in honesty, or at all in

306

K

108 Old Style Minion

109 Old Style Nonpareil

A book is essentially not a talked thing, but a written thing; and written, not with a view of mere communication, but of permanence. The book of talk is printed only because its author cannot speak to thousands of people at once; if he could, he would—the volume is mere multiplication of his voice. You cannot talk to your friend in India; if you could, you would; you write instead: that is mere conveyance of voice. But a book is written, not to multiply the voice merely, not to carry it merely, but to perpetuate it. The author has something to say which he perceives to be true and useful, or helpfully beautiful. So far as he knows, no one has yet said it; so far as he knows, no one else can say it. He is bound to say it, clearly and melodiously if he may; clearly, at all events. In the sum of his life he finds this to be the thing, or group of things, manifest to him;—this, the piece of true knowledge, or sight, which his share of sunshine and earth has permitted him to seize. He would fain set it down for ever; engrave it on rock, if he could; saying, "This is the best of me; for the rest, I ate, and drank, and slept, loved, and hated, like another; my life was as the vapour, and is not; but this I saw and knew: this, if anything of mine, is worth your memory." That is his "writing"; it is, in his small human way, and with whatever degree of true inspiration is in him, his inscription, or scripture. That is a

280

A book is essentially not a talked thing, but a written thing; and written, not with a view of mere communication, but of permanence. The book of talk is printed only because its author cannot speak to thousands of people at once; if he could, he would—the volume is mere multiplication of his voice. You cannot talk to your friend in India; if you could, you would; you write instead: that is mere conveyance of voice. But a book is written, not to multiply the voice merely, not to carry it merely, but to perpetuate it. The author has something to say which he perceives to be true and useful, or helpfully beautiful. So far as he knows, no one has yet said it; so far as he knows, no one else can say it. He is bound to say it, clearly and melodiously if he may; clearly, at all events. In the sum of his life he finds this to be the thing, or group of things, manifest to him;—this, the piece of true knowledge, or sight, which his share of sunshine and earth has permitted him to seize. He would fain set it down for ever; engrave it on rock, if he could; saying, "This is the best of me; for the rest, I ate, and drank, and slept, loved, and hated, like another; my life was as the vapour, and is not; but this I saw and knew: this, if anything of mine, is worth your memory." That is his "writing"; it is, in his small human way, and with whatever degree of true inspiration is in him, his inscription, or scripture. That is a "Book." Perhaps you think no books were ever so written? But, again, I ask you, do you at all believe in honesty, or at all in kindness? or do you think there is never any honesty or benevolence in wise people? None of us, I hope, are so unhappy as to think

332

A book is essentially not a talked thing, but a written thing; and written, not with a view of mere communication, but of permanence. The book of talk is printed only because its author cannot speak to thousands of people at once; if he could, he would—the volume is mere multiplication of his voice. You cannot talk to your friend in India; if you could, you would; you write instead: that is mere conveyance of voice. But a book is written, not to multiply the voice merely, not to carry it merely, but to perpetuate it. The author has something to say which he perceives to be true and useful, or helpfully beautiful. So far as he knows, no one has yet said it; so far as he knows, no one else can say it. He is bound to say it, clearly and melodiously if he may; clearly, at all events. In the sum of his life he finds this to be the thing, or group of things, manifest to him;—this, the piece of true knowledge, or sight, which his share of sunshine and earth has permitted him to seize. He would fain set it down for ever; engrave it on rock, if he could; saying, "This is the best of me; for the rest, I ate, and drank, and slept, loved, and hated, like another; my life was as the vapour, and is not; but this I saw and knew: this, if anything of mine, is worth your memory." That is his "writing"; it is, in his small human way, and with whatever degree of true inspiration is in him, his inscription, or scripture. That is a "Book." Perhaps you think no books were ever so written? But, again, I ask you, do you at all believe in honesty, or at all in kindness? or do you think there is never any honesty or benevolence in wise people? None of us, I hope, are so unhappy as to think that. Well, whatever bit of a wise man's work is honestly and benevolently done, that bit is his book, or his piece of art. It is mixed always with evil fragments—ill-done, redundant, affected work. But if you read rightly, you will easily discover the true bits, and those are the book. Now, books of this kind have been written in all ages by their greatest men,—by great readers, great statesmen, and great thinkers. These are all at

412

A book is essentially not a talked thing, but a written thing; and written, not with a view of mere communication, but of permanence. The book of talk is printed only because its author cannot speak to thousands of people at once; if he could, he would—the volume is mere multiplication of his voice. You cannot talk to your friend in India; if you could, you would; you write instead: that is mere conveyance of voice. But a book is written, not to multiply the voice merely, not to carry it merely, but to perpetuate it. The author has something to say which he perceives to be true and useful, or helpfully beautiful. So far as he knows, no one has yet said it; so far as he knows, no one else can say it. He is bound to say it, clearly and melodiously if he may; clearly, at all events. In the sum of his life he finds this to be the thing, or group of things, manifest to him;—this, the piece of true knowledge, or sight, which his share of sunshine and earth has permitted him to seize. He would fain set it down for ever; engrave it on rock, if he could; saying, "This is the best of me; for the rest, I ate, and drank, and slept, loved, and hated, like another; my life was as the vapour, and is not; but this I saw and knew: this, if anything of mine, is worth your memory." That is his "writing"; it is, in his small human way, and with whatever degree of true inspiration is in him, his inscription, or scripture. That is a "Book." Perhaps you think no books were ever so written? But, again, I ask you, do you at all believe in honesty, or at all in kindness? or do you think there is never any honesty or benevolence in wise people? None of us, I hope, are so unhappy as to think that. Well, whatever bit of a wise man's work is honestly and benevolently done, that bit is his book, or his piece of art. It is mixed always with evil fragments—ill-done, redundant, affected work. But if you read rightly, you will easily discover the true bits, and those are

383

A book is essentially not a talked thing, but a written thing; and written, not with a view of mere communication, but of permanence. The book of talk is printed only because its author cannot speak to thousands of people at once; if he could, he would—the volume is mere multiplication of his voice. You cannot talk to your friend in India; if you could, you would; you write instead: that is mere conveyance of voice. But a book is written, not to multiply the voice merely, not to carry it merely, but to perpetuate it. The author has something to say which he perceives to be true and useful, or helpfully beautiful. So far as he knows, no one has yet said it; so far as he knows, no one else can say it. He is bound to say it, clearly and melodiously if he may; clearly, at all events. In the sum of his life he finds this to be the thing, or group of things, manifest to him;—this, the piece of true knowledge, or sight, which his share of sunshine and earth has permitted him to seize. He would fain set it down for ever; engrave it on rock, if he could; saying, "This is the best of me; for the rest, I ate, and drank, and slept, loved, and hated, like another; my life was as the vapour, and is not; but this I saw and knew: this, if anything of mine, is worth your memory." That is his "writing"; it is, in his small human way, and with whatever degree of true inspiration is in him, his inscription, or scripture. That is a "Book." Perhaps you think no books were ever so written? But, again, I ask you, do you at all believe in honesty, or at all in kindness? or do you think there is never any honesty or benevolence in wise people? None of us, I hope, are so unhappy as to think that. Well, whatever bit of a wise man's work is honestly and benevolently done, that bit is his book, or his piece of art. It is mixed always with evil fragments—ill-done, redundant, affected work. But if you read rightly, you will easily discover the true bits, and those are the book. Now, books of this kind have been written in all ages by their greatest men,—by great readers, great statesmen, and great thinkers. These are all at your choice; and Life is short. You have heard as much before;—yet have you measured and mapped out this short life and its possibilities Do you know, if you read this, that you cannot read that—that what you lose to-day you cannot gain

458

A book is essentially not a talked thing, but a written thing; and written, not with a view of mere communication, but of permanence. The book of talk is printed only because its author cannot speak to thousands of people at once; if he could, he would—the volume is mere multiplication of his voice. You cannot talk to your friend in India; if you could, you would; you write instead: that is mere conveyance of voice. But a book is written, not to multiply the voice merely, not to carry it merely, but to perpetuate it. The author has something to say which he perceives to be true and useful, or helpfully beautiful. So far as he knows, no one has yet said it; so far as he knows, no one else can say it. He is bound to say it, clearly and melodiously if he may; clearly, at all events. In the sum of his life he finds this to be the thing, or group of things, manifest to him;—this, the piece of true knowledge, or sight, which his share of sunshine and earth has permitted him to seize. He would fain set it down for ever; engrave it on rock, if he could; saying, "This is the best of me; for the rest, I ate, and drank, and slept, loved, and hated, like another; my life was as the vapour, and is not; but this I saw and knew: this, if anything of mine, is worth your memory." That is his "writing"; it is, in his small human way, and with whatever degree of true inspiration is in him, his inscription, or scripture. That is a "Book." Perhaps you think no books were ever so written? But, again, I ask you, do you at all believe in honesty, or at all in kindness? or do you think there is never any honesty or benevolence in wise people? None of us, I hope, are so unhappy as to think that. Well, whatever bit of a wise man's work is honestly and benevolently done, that bit is his book, or his piece of art. It is mixed always with evil fragments—ill-done, redundant, affected work. But if you read rightly, you will easily discover the true bits, and those are the book. Now, books of this kind have been written in all ages by their greatest men,—by great readers, great statesmen, and great thinkers. These are all at your choice; and Life is short. You have heard as much before;—yet have you measured and mapped out this short life and its possibilities? Do you know, if you read this, that you cannot read that—that what you lose to-day you cannot gain to-morrow? Will you go and gossip with your housemaid, or your stable-boy, when you may talk with queens and kings; or flatter yourselves that it is with any worthy consciousness of your own claims to respect, that you jostle with the hungry and common crowd for entrée here, and audience there, when all the while this eternal court is open to you, with its society, wide as the world, multitudinous as its days, the chosen, and the mighty, of every place and time? Into that you may enter always; in that you may take fellowship and rank according to your wish; from that, once entered into it, you can

569

K 2

110 Old Style Pearl

111 Antique Great Primer

A book is essentially not a talked thing, but a written thing; and written, not with a view of mere communication, but of permanence. The book of talk is printed only because its author cannot speak to

37

A book is essentially not a talked thing, but a written thing; and written, not with a view of mere communication, but of permanence. The book of talk is printed only because its author cannot speak to thousands of people at once;

42

A book is essentially not a talked thing, but a written thing; and written, not with a view of mere communication, but of permanence. The book of talk is printed only because its author cannot speak to thousands of people at once; if he could, he would—the vol-

49

A book is essentially not a talked thing, but a written thing; and written, not with a view of mere communication, but of permanence. The book of talk is printed only because its author cannot speak to thousands of people at once; if he could, he would—the volume is mere multiplication of his voice. You cannot talk to your friend in India; if you could, you would; you write instead: that is mere conveyance of voice. But a

A book is essentially not a talked thing, but a written thing; and written, not with a view of mere communication, but of permanence. The book of talk is printed only because its author cannot speak to thousands of people at once; if he could, he would—the volume is mere multiplication of his voice. You cannot talk to your friend in India; if you could, you would; you write instead: that is mere conveyance of voice. But a book is written, not to multiply the voice

A book is essentially not a talked thing, but a written thing; and written, not with a view of mere communication, but of permanence. The book of talk is printed only because its author cannot speak to thousands of people at once; if he could, he would—the volume is mere multiplication of his voice. You cannot talk to your friend in India; if you could, you would; you write instead: that is mere conveyance of voice. But a book is written, not to multiply the voice merely, not to carry it merely, but to per-

113 Antique Long Primer

A book is essentially not a talked thing, but a written thing; and written, not with a view of mere communication, but of permanence. The book of talk is printed only because its author cannot speak to thousands of people at once; if he could, he would— the volume is mere multiplication of his voice. You cannot talk to your friend in India; if you could, you would; you write instead: that is mere conveyance of voice. But a book is written, not to multiply the voice merely, not to carry it merely, but to perpetuate it. The author has something to say which he perceives to be true and useful, or helpfully beau-

114

A book is essentially not a talked thing, but a written thing; and written, not with a view of mere communication, but of permanence. The book of talk is printed only because its author cannot speak to thousands of people at once; if he could, he would— the volume is mere multiplication of his voice. You cannot talk to your friend in India; if you could, you would; you write instead: that is mere conveyance of voice. But a book is written, not to multiply the voice merely, not to carry it merely, but to perpetuate it. The author has something to say which he perceives to be true and useful, or helpfully beautiful. So far as he knows, no one has yet said it; so far as he knows, no one else can say it. He is bound

139

A book is essentially not a talked thing, but a written thing; and written, not with a view of mere communication, but of permanence. The book of talk is printed only because its author cannot speak to thousands of people at once; if he could, he would— the volume is mere multiplication of his voice. You cannot talk to your friend in India; if you could, you would; you write instead: that is mere conveyance of voice. But a book is written, not to multiply the voice merely, not to carry it merely, but to perpetuate it. The author has something to say which he perceives to be true and useful, or helpfully beautiful. So far as he knows, no one has yet said it; so far as he knows, no one else can say it. He is bound to say it, clearly and melodiously if he may; clearly, at all events. In the sum of his life he finds this to

162

A book is essentially not a talked thing, but a written thing; and written, not with a view of mere communication, but of permanence. The book of talk is printed only because its author cannot speak to thousands of people at once; if he could, he would—the volume is mere multiplication of his voice. You cannot talk to your friend in India; if you could, you would; you write instead: that is mere conveyance of voice. But a book is written, not to multiply the voice merely, not to carry it merely, but to perpetuate it. The author has something to say which he perceives to be true and useful, or helpfully beautiful. So far as he knows, no one has yet said it; so far as he knows, no one else can say it. He is bound to say it, clearly and melodiously if he may; clearly, at all events. In the sum of his life he finds this to be the thing, or group of things, manifest to him;—this, the piece of true knowledge, or

179

A book is essentially not a talked thing, but a written thing; and written, not with a view of mere communication, but of permanence. The book of talk is printed only because its author cannot speak to thousands of people at once; if he could, he would—the volume is mere multiplication of his voice. You cannot talk to your friend in India; if you could, you would; you write instead: that is mere conveyance of voice. But a book is written, not to multiply the voice merely, not to carry it merely, but to perpetuate it. The author has something to say which he perceives to be true and useful, or helpfully beautiful. So far as he knows, no one has yet said it; so far as he knows, no one else can say it. He is bound to say it, clearly and melodiously if he may; clearly, at all events. In the sum of his life he finds this to be the thing, or group of things, manifest to him;—this, the piece of true knowledge, or sight, which his share of sunshine and earth has permitted him to seize. He would fain set it down for ever; engrave it on rock, if

205

A book is essentially not a talked thing, but a written thing; and written, not with a view of mere communication, but of permanence. The book of talk is printed only because its author cannot speak to thousands of people at once; if he could, he would—the volume is mere multiplication of his voice. You cannot talk to your friend in India; if you could, you would; you write instead: that is mere conveyance of voice. But a book is written, not to multiply the voice merely, not to carry it merely, but to perpetuate it. The author has something to say which he perceives to be true and useful, or helpfully beautiful. So far as he knows, no one has yet said it; so far as he knows, no one else can say it. He is bound to say it, clearly and melodiously if he may; clearly, at all events. In the sum of his life he finds this to be the thing, or group of things, manifest to him;—this, the piece of true knowledge, or sight, which his share of sunshine and earth has permitted him to seize. He would fain set it down for ever; engrave it on rock, if he could; saying, "This is the best of me; for the rest, I ate, and drank, and slept, loved, and hated, like another; my life was as the

233

114 Antique Brevier

115 Antique Nonpareil

A book is essentially not a talked thing, but a written thing; and written, not with a view of mere communication, but of permanence. The book of talk is printed only because its author cannot speak to thousands of people at once; if he could, he would—the volume is mere multiplication of his voice. You cannot talk to your friend in India; if you could, you would; you write instead: that is mere conveyance of voice. But a book is written, not to multiply the voice merely, not to carry it merely, but to perpetuate it. The author has something to say which he perceives to be true and useful, or helpfully beautiful. So far as he knows, no one has yet said it; so far as he knows, no one else can say it. He is bound to say it, clearly and melodiously if he may; clearly, at all events. In the sum of his life he finds this to be the thing, or group of things, manifest to him;—this, the piece of true knowledge, or sight, which his share of sunshine and earth has permitted him to seize. He would fain set it down for ever; engrave it on rock, if he could; saying, " This is the best of me; for the rest, I ate, and drank, and slept, loved, and hated, like another; my life was as the vapour, and is not; but this I saw and knew: this, if anything of mine, is worth your memory."

252

A book is essentially not a talked thing, but a written thing; and written, not with a view of mere communication, but of permanence. The book of talk is printed only because its author cannot speak to thousands of people at once; if he could, he would—the volume is mere multiplication of his voice. You cannot talk to your friend in India; if you could, you would; you write instead: that is mere conveyance of voice. But a book is written, not to multiply the voice merely, not to carry it merely, but to perpetuate it. The author has something to say which he perceives to be true and useful, or helpfully beautiful. So far as he knows, no one has yet said it; so far as he knows, no one else can say it. He is bound to say it, clearly and melodiously if he may; clearly, at all events. In the sum of his life he finds this to be the thing, or group of things, manifest to him;—this, the piece of true knowledge, or sight, which his share of sunshine and earth has permitted him to seize. He would fain set it down for ever; engrave it on rock, if he could; saying, " This is the best of me; for the rest, I ate, and drank, and slept, loved, and hated, like another; my life was as the vapour, and is not; but this I saw and knew: this, if anything of mine, is worth your memory." That is his " writing "; it is, in his small human way, and with whatever degree of true inspiration is in him, his inscription, or scripture. That is a "Book." Perhaps you think no books were ever so written? But, again, I ask you, do you

297

A book is essentially not a talked thing, but a written thing; and written, not with a view of mere communication, but of permanence. The book of talk is printed only because its author cannot speak to thousands of people at once; if he could, he would—the volume is mere multiplication of his voice. You cannot talk to your friend in India; if you could, you would; you write instead: that is mere conveyance of voice. But a book is written, not to multiply the voice merely, not to carry it merely, but to perpetuate it. The author has something to say which he perceives to be true and useful, or helpfully beautiful. So far as he knows, no one has yet said it; so far as he knows, no one else can say it. He is bound to say it, clearly and melodiously if he may; clearly, at all events. In the sum of his life he finds this to be the thing, or group of things, manifest to him;—this, the piece of true knowledge, or sight, which his share of sunshine and earth has permitted him to seize. He would fain set it down for ever; engrave it on rock, if he could; saying, " This is the best of me; for the rest, I ate, and drank, and slept, loved, and hated, like another; my life was as the vapour, and is not; but this I saw and knew: this, if anything of mine, is worth your memory." That is his " writing "; it is, in his small human way, and with whatever degree of true inspiration is in him, his inscription, or scripture. That is a "Book." Perhaps you think no books were ever so written? But, again, I ask you, do you at all believe in honesty, or at all in kindness? or do you think there is never any honesty or benevolence in wise people? None of us, I hope, are so unhappy as to think that. Well, whatever bit of a wise man's work is honestly and benevolently done, that bit is his book, or his piece of art. It is mixed always with evil fragments—ill-done, redundant, affected work. But if you read rightly, you

374

A book is essentially not a talked thing, but a written thing; and written, not with a view of mere communication, but of permanence. The book of talk is printed only because its author cannot speak to thousands of people at once; if he

44

A book is essentially not a talked thing, but a written thing; and written, not with a view of mere communication, but of permanence. The book of talk is printed only because its author cannot speak to thousands of people at once; if he could, he would—the volume is

50

A book is essentially not a talked thing, but a written thing; and written, not with a view of mere communication, but of permanence. The book of talk is printed only because its author cannot speak to thousands of people at once; if he could, he would—the volume is mere multiplication of his voice.

55

L

116 Modern Great Primer

A book is essentially not a talked thing, but a written thing; and written, not with a view of mere communication, but of permanence. The book of talk is printed only because its author cannot speak to thousands of people at once; if he could, he would—the volume is mere multiplication of his voice. You cannot talk to your friend in India; if you could, you would;

68

A book is essentially not a talked thing, but a written thing; and written, not with a view of mere communication, but of permanence. The book of talk is printed only because its author cannot speak to thousands of people at once; if he could, he would—the volume is mere multiplication of his voice. You cannot talk to your friend in India; if you could, you would; you write instead: that is mere conveyance

75

A book is essentially not a talked thing, but a written thing; and written, not with a view of mere communication, but of permanence. The book of talk is printed only because its author cannot speak to thousands of people at once; if he could, he would—the volume is mere multiplication of his voice. You cannot talk to your friend in India; if you could, you would; you write instead: that is mere conveyance of voice. But a book is written, not to

84

A book is essentially not a talked thing, but a written thing ; and written, not with a view of mere communication, but of permanence. The book of talk is printed only because its author cannot speak to thousands of people at once ; if he could, he would—the volume is mere multiplication of his voice. You cannot talk to your friend in India ; if you could, you would ; you write instead : that is mere conveyance of voice. But a book is written, not to multiply the voice

87

A book is essentially not a talked thing, but a written thing ; and written, not with a view of mere communication, but of permanence. The book of talk is printed only because its author cannot speak to thousands of people at once ; if he could, he would—the volume is mere multiplication of his voice. You cannot talk to your friend in India ; if you could, you would ; you write instead : that is mere conveyance of voice. But a book is written, not to multiply the voice merely, not to carry it merely, but to perpetuate

96

A book is essentially not a talked thing, but a written thing ; and written, not with a view of mere communication, but of permanence. The book of talk is printed only because its author cannot speak to thousands of people at once ; if he could, he would—the volume is mere multiplication of his voice. You cannot talk to your friend in India ; if you could, you would ; you write instead : that is mere conveyance of voice. But a book is written, not to multiply the voice merely, not to carry it merely, but to perpetuate it. The author has something to say which he

118 Modern Pica

119 Modern Small Pica

A book is essentially not a talked thing, but a written thing; and written, not with a view of mere communication, but of permanence. The book of talk is printed only because its author cannot speak to thousands of people at once; if he could, he would—the volume is mere multiplication of his voice. You cannot talk to your friend in India; if you could, you would; you write instead: that is mere conveyance of voice. But a book is written, not to multiply the voice merely, not to carry it merely, but to perpetuate it. The author has something to say which he perceives to be true and

110

A book is essentially not a talked thing, but a written thing; and written, not with a view of mere communication, but of permanence. The book of talk is printed only because its author cannot speak to thousands of people at once; if he could, he would—the volume is mere multiplication of his voice. You cannot talk to your friend in India; if you could, you would; you write instead: that is mere conveyance of voice. But a book is written, not to multiply the voice merely, not to carry it merely, but to perpetuate it. The author has something to say which he perceives to be true and useful, or helpfully beautiful. So far as he knows, no one has yet said it; so far as he knows, no one else can

134

A book is essentially not a talked thing, but a written thing; and written, not with a view of mere communication, but of permanence. The book of talk is printed only because its author cannot speak to thousands of people at once; if he could, he would—the volume is mere multiplication of his voice. You cannot talk to your friend in India; if you could, you would; you write instead: that is mere conveyance of voice. But a book is written, not to multiply the voice merely, not to carry it merely, but to perpetuate it. The author has something to say which he perceives to be true and useful, or helpfully beautiful. So far as he knows, no one has yet said it; so far as he knows, no one else can say it. He is bound to say it, clearly and melodiously if he may; clearly, at all events. In the sum of his life

158

A book is essentially not a talked thing, but a written thing; and written, not with a view of mere communication, but of permanence. The book of talk is printed only because its author cannot speak to thousands of people at once; if he could, he would—the volume is mere multiplication of his voice. You cannot talk to your friend in India; if you could, you would; you write instead: that is mere conveyance of voice. But a book is written, not to multiply the voice merely, not to carry it merely, but to perpetuate it. The author has something to say which he perceives to be true and useful, or helpfully beautiful. So far as he knows, no one has yet said it; so far as he knows, no one else can say it. He is bound

139

A book is essentially not a talked thing, but a written thing; and written, not with a view of mere communication, but of permanence. The book of talk is printed only because its author cannot speak to thousands of people at once; if he could, he would—the volume is mere multiplication of his voice. You cannot talk to your friend in India; if you could, you would; you write instead: that is mere conveyance of voice. But a book is written, not to multiply the voice merely, not to carry it merely, but to perpetuate it. The author has something to say which he perceives to be true and useful, or helpfully beautiful. So far as he knows, no one has yet said it; so far as he knows, no one else can say it. He is bound to say it, clearly and melodiously if he may; clearly, at all events. In the sum of his life he finds this to be the thing,

165

A book is essentially not a talked thing, but a written thing; and written, not with a view of mere communication, but of permanence. The book of talk is printed only because its author cannot speak to thousands of people at once; if he could, he would—the volume is mere multiplication of his voice. You cannot talk to your friend in India; if you could, you would; you write instead: that is mere conveyance of voice. But a book is written, not to multiply the voice merely, not to carry it merely, but to perpetuate it. The author has something to say which he perceives to be true and useful, or helpfully beautiful. So far as he knows, no one has yet said it; so far as he knows, no one else can say it. He is bound to say it, clearly and melodiously if he may; clearly, at all events. In the sum of his life he finds this to be the thing, or group of things, manifest to him;—this, the piece of true knowledge, or sight, which his share of sunshine and earth

187

120 Modern Long Primer

121 Modern Bourgeois

A book is essentially not a talked thing, but a written thing; and written, not with a view of mere communication, but of permanence. The book of talk is printed only because its author cannot speak to thousands of people at once; if he could, he would—the volume is mere multiplication of his voice. You cannot talk to your friend in India; if you could, you would; you write instead: that is mere conveyance of voice. But a book is written, not to multiply the voice merely, not to carry it merely, but to perpetuate it. The author has something to say which he perceives to be true and useful, or helpfully beautiful. So far as he knows, no one has yet said it; so far as he knows, no one else can say it. He is bound to say it, clearly and melodiously if he may; clearly, at all events. In the sum of his life he finds this to be the thing, or group of

168

A book is essentially not a talked thing, but a written thing; and written, not with a view of mere communication, but of permanence. The book of talk is printed only because its author cannot speak to thousands of people at once; if he could, he would—the volume is mere multiplication of his voice. You cannot talk to your friend in India; if you could, you would; you write instead: that is mere conveyance of voice. But a book is written, not to multiply the voice merely, not to carry it merely, but to perpetuate it. The author has something to say which he perceives to be true and useful, or helpfully beautiful. So far as he knows, no one has yet said it; so far as he knows, no one else can say it. He is bound to say it, clearly and melodiously if he may; clearly, at all events. In the sum of his life he finds this to be the thing, or group of things, manifest to him;—this, the piece of true knowledge, or sight, which his share of sunshine and earth has permitted him to

191

A book is essentially not a talked thing, but a written thing; and written, not with a view of mere communication, but of permanence. The book of talk is printed only because its author cannot speak to thousands of people at once; if he could, he would—the volume is mere multiplication of his voice. You cannot talk to your friend in India; if you could, you would; you write instead: that is mere conveyance of voice. But a book is written, not to multiply the voice merely, not to carry it merely, but to perpetuate it. The author has something to say which he perceives to be true and useful, or helpfully beautiful. So far as he knows, no one has yet said it; so far as he knows, no one else can say it. He is bound to say it, clearly and melodiously if he may; clearly, at all events. In the sum of his life he finds this to be the thing, or group of things, manifest to him;—this, the piece of true knowledge, or sight, which his share of sunshine and earth has permitted him to seize. He would fain set it down for ever; engrave it on rock, if he could; saying, "This is the best of me; for the rest, I ate, and

220

A book is essentially not a talked thing, but a written thing; and written, not with a view of mere communication, but of permanence. The book of talk is printed only because its author cannot speak to thousands of people at once; if he could, he would—the volume is mere multiplication of his voice. You cannot talk to your friend in India; if you could, you would; you write instead: that is mere conveyance of voice. But a book is written, not to multiply the voice merely, not to carry it merely, but to perpetuate it. The author has something to say which he perceives to be true and useful, or helpfully beautiful. So far as he knows, no one has yet said it; so far as he knows, no one else can say it. He is bound to say it, clearly and melodiously if he may; clearly, at all events. In the sum of his life he finds this to be the thing, or group of things, manifest to him;— this, the piece of true knowledge, or sight, which his share of sunshine
185

A book is essentially not a talked thing, but a written thing; and written, not with a view of mere communication, but of permanence. The book of talk is printed only because its author cannot speak to thousands of people at once; if he could, he would—the volume is mere multiplication of his voice. You cannot talk to your friend in India; if you could, you would; you write instead: that is mere conveyance of voice. But a book is written, not to multiply the voice merely, not to carry it merely, but to perpetuate it. The author has something to say which he perceives to be true and useful, or helpfully beautiful. So far as he knows, no one has yet said it; so far as he knows, no one else can say it. He is bound to say it, clearly and melodiously if he may; clearly, at all events. In the sum of his life he finds this to be the thing, or group of things, manifest to him;— this, the piece of true knowledge, or sight, which his share of sunshine and earth has permitted him to seize. He would fain set it down for ever; engrave it on rock, if he could; saying, "This is the best of me;
214

A book is essentially not a talked thing, but a written thing; and written, not with a view of mere communication, but of permanence. The book of talk is printed only because its author cannot speak to thousands of people at once; if he could, he would—the volume is mere multiplication of his voice. You cannot talk to your friend in India; if you could, you would; you write instead: that is mere conveyance of voice. But a book is written, not to multiply the voice merely, not to carry it merely, but to perpetuate it. The author has something to say which he perceives to be true and useful, or helpfully beautiful. So far as he knows, no one has yet said it; so far as he knows, no one else can say it. He is bound to say it, clearly and melodiously if he may; clearly, at all events. In the sum of his life he finds this to be the thing, or group of things, manifest to him;— this, the piece of true knowledge, or sight, which his share of sunshine and earth has permitted him to seize. He would fain set it down for ever; engrave it on rock, if he could; saying, "This is the best of me; for the rest, I ate, and drank, and slept, loved, and hated, like another; my life was as the vapour, and is not; but this I saw and knew: this,
244

123 Modern Minion

A book is essentially not a talked thing, but a written thing; and written, not with a view of mere communication, but of permanence. The book of talk is printed only because its author cannot speak to thousands of people at once; if he could, he would—the volume is mere multiplication of his voice. You cannot talk to your friend in India; if you could, you would; you write instead: that is mere conveyance of voice. But a book is written, not to multiply the voice merely, not to carry it merely, but to perpetuate it. The author has something to say which he perceives to be true and useful, or helpfully beautiful. So far as he knows, no one has yet said it; so far as he knows, no one else can say it. He is bound to say it, clearly and melodiously if he may; clearly, at all events. In the sum of his life he finds this to be the thing, or group of things, manifest to him;—this, the piece of true knowledge, or sight, which his share of sunshine and earth has permitted him to seize. He would fain set it down for ever; engrave it on rock, if he could; saying, "This is the best of me; for the rest, I ate, and drank, and slept, loved, and hated, like

227

A book is essentially not a talked thing, but a written thing; and written, not with a view of mere communication, but of permanence. The book of talk is printed only because its author cannot speak to thousands of people at once; if he could, he would—the volume is mere multiplication of his voice. You cannot talk to your friend in India; if you could, you would; you write instead: that is mere conveyance of voice. But a book is written, not to multiply the voice merely, not to carry it merely, but to perpetuate it. The author has something to say which he perceives to be true and useful, or helpfully beautiful. So far as he knows, no one has yet said it; so far as he knows, no one else can say it. He is bound to say it, clearly and melodiously if he may; clearly, at all events. In the sum of his life he finds this to be the thing, or group of things, manifest to him;—this, the piece of true knowledge, or sight, which his share of sunshine and earth has permitted him to seize. He would fain set it down for ever; engrave it on rock, if he could; saying, "This is the best of me; for the rest, I ate, and drank, and slept, loved, and hated, like another; my life was as the vapour, and is not; but this I saw and knew: this, if anything of mine, is worth your memory." That is his "writing"; it

257

A book is essentially not a talked thing, but a written thing; and written, not with a view of mere communication, but of permanence. The book of talk is printed only because its author cannot speak to thousands of people at once; if he could, he would—the volume is mere multiplication of his voice. You cannot talk to your friend in India; if you could, you would; you write instead: that is mere conveyance of voice. But a book is written, not to multiply the voice merely, not to carry it merely, but to perpetuate it. The author has something to say which he perceives to be true and useful, or helpfully beautiful. So far as he knows, no one has yet said it; so far as he knows, no one else can say it. He is bound to say it, clearly and melodiously if he may; clearly, at all events. In the sum of his life he finds this to be the thing, or group of things, manifest to him;—this, the piece of true knowledge, or sight, which his share of sunshine and earth has permitted him to seize. He would fain set it down for ever; engrave it on rock, if he could; saying, "This is the best of me; for the rest, I ate, and drank, and slept, loved, and hated, like another; my life was as the vapour, and is not; but this I saw and knew: this, if anything of mine, is worth your memory." That is his "writing"; it is, in his small human way, and with whatever degree of true inspiration is in him, his inscription, or scripture. That is a "Book." Perhaps you think no books were ever so written? But, again, I ask you, do you at all believe in

301

A book is essentially not a talked thing, but a written thing ; and written, not with a view of mere communication, but of permanence. The book of talk is printed only because its author cannot speak to thousands of people at once ; if he could, he would—the volume is mere multiplication of his voice. You cannot talk to your friend in India ; if you could, you would ; you write instead : that is mere conveyance of voice. But a book is written, not to multiply the voice merely, not to carry it merely, but to perpetuate it. The author has something to say which he perceives to be true and useful, or helpfully beautiful. So far as he knows, no one has yet said it ; so far as he knows, no one else can say it. He is bound to say it, clearly and melodiously if he may ; clearly, at all events. In the sum of his life he finds this to be the thing, or group of things, manifest to him ;—this, the piece of true knowledge, or sight, which his share of sunshine and earth has permitted him to seize. He would fain set it down for ever ; engrave it on rock, if he could ; saying, "This is the best of me ; for the rest, I ate, and drank, and slept, loved, and hated, like another ; my life was as the vapour, and is not ; but this I saw and knew : this, if anything of mine, is worth your memory." That is his "writing" ; it is, in his
260

A book is essentially not a talked thing, but a written thing ; and written, not with a view of mere communication, but of permanence. The book of talk is printed only because its author cannot speak to thousands of people at once ; if he could, he would—the volume is mere multiplication of his voice. You cannot talk to your friend in India ; if you could, you would ; you write instead : that is mere conveyance of voice. But a book is written, not to multiply the voice merely, not to carry it merely, but to perpetuate it. The author has something to say which he perceives to be true and useful, or helpfully beautiful. So far as he knows, no one has yet said it ; so far as he knows, no one else can say it. He is bound to say it, clearly and melodiously if he may ; clearly, at all events. In the sum of his life he finds this to be the thing, or group of things, manifest to him ;—this, the piece of true knowledge, or sight, which his share of sunshine and earth has permitted him to seize. He would fain set it down for ever ; engrave it on rock, if he could ; saying, "This is the best of me ; for the rest, I ate, and drank, and slept, loved, and hated, like another ; my life was as the vapour, and is not ; but this I saw and knew : this, if anything of mine, is worth your memory." That is his "writing" ; it is, in his small human way, and with whatever degree of true inspiration is in him, his inscription, or scripture. That is a "Book." Perhaps you think no books were ever so written ? But, again, I ask you, do you at all believe in honesty, or at all in
306

A book is essentially not a talked thing, but a written thing ; and written, not with a view of mere communication, but of permanence. The book of talk is printed only because its author cannot speak to thousands of people at once ; if he could, he would—the volume is mere multiplication of his voice. You cannot talk to your friend in India ; if you could, you would ; you write instead : that is mere conveyance of voice. But a book is written, not to multiply the voice merely, not to carry it merely, but to perpetuate it. The author has something to say which he perceives to be true and useful, or helpfully beautiful. So far as he knows, no one has yet said it ; so far as he knows, no one else can say it. He is bound to say it, clearly and melodiously if he may ; clearly, at all events. In the sum of his life he finds this to be the thing, or group of things, manifest to him ;—this, the piece of true knowledge, or sight, which his share of sunshine and earth has permitted him to seize. He would fain set it down for ever ; engrave it on rock, if he could ; saying, "This is the best of me ; for the rest, I ate, and drank, and slept, loved, and hated, like another ; my life was as the vapour, and is not ; but this I saw and knew : this, if anything of mine, is worth your memory." That is his "writing" ; it is, in his small human way, and with whatever degree of true inspiration is in him, his inscription, or scripture. That is a "Book." Perhaps you think no books were ever so written ? But, again, I ask you, do you at all believe in honesty, or at all in kindness ? or do you think there is never any honesty or benevolence in wise people ? None of us, I hope, are so unhappy as to think that. Well, whatever bit of a wise man's work is honestly and benevolently done, that bit is his book, or his piece of art. It is mixed always with evil fragments—ill-done, redundant, affected work. But if you read rightly, you will easily discover the true bits, and those are the book.
385

M

A book is essentially not a talked thing, but a written thing; and written, not with a view of mere communication, but of permanence. The book of talk is printed only because its author cannot speak to thousands of people at once; if he could, he would—the volume is mere multiplication of his voice. You cannot talk to your friend in India; if you could, you would; you write instead: that is mere conveyance of voice. But a book is written, not to multiply the voice merely, not to carry it merely, but to perpetuate it. The author has something to say which he perceives to be true and useful, or helpfully beautiful. So far as he knows, no one has yet said it; so far as he knows, no one else can say it. He is bound to say it, clearly and melodiously if he may; clearly, at all events. In the sum of his life he finds this to be the thing, or group of things, manifest to him; —this, the piece of true knowledge, or sight, which his share of sunshine and earth has permitted him to seize. He would fain set it down for ever; engrave it on rock, if he could; saying, "This is the best of me; for the rest, I ate, and drank, and slept, loved, and hated, like another; my life was as the vapour, and is not; but this I saw and knew: this, if anything of mine, is worth your memory." That is his "writing"; it is, in his small human way, and with whatever degree of true inspiration is in him, his inscription, or scripture. That is a "Book." Perhaps you think no books were ever so written? But, again, I ask you, do you at all believe in honesty, or at all in kindness? or do you think there is never any honesty or benevolence in wise people? None of us, I hope, are so unhappy as to think that. Well, whatever bit of a wise man's work is honestly and benevolently done, that bit is his book, or his piece of art. It is mixed always with evil fragments—ill-done,

365

A book is essentially not a talked thing, but a written thing; and written, not with a view of mere communication, but of permanence. The book of talk is printed only because its author cannot speak to thousands of people at once; if he could, he would—the volume is mere multiplication of his voice. You cannot talk to your friend in India; if you could, you would; you write instead: that is mere conveyance of voice. But a book is written, not to multiply the voice merely, not to carry it merely, but to perpetuate it. The author has something to say which he perceives to be true and useful, or helpfully beautiful. So far as he knows, no one has yet said it; so far as he knows, no one else can say it. He is bound to say it, clearly and melodiously if he may; clearly, at all events. In the sum of his life he finds this to be the thing, or group of things, manifest to him; —this, the piece of true knowledge, or sight, which his share of sunshine and earth has permitted him to seize. He would fain set it down for ever; engrave it on rock, if he could; saying, "This is the best of me; for the rest, I ate, and drank, and slept, loved, and hated, like another; my life was as the vapour, and is not; but this I saw and knew: this, if anything of mine, is worth your memory." That is his "writing"; it is, in his small human way, and with whatever degree of true inspiration is in him, his inscription, or scripture. That is a "Book." Perhaps you think no books were ever so written? But, again, I ask you, do you at all believe in honesty, or at all in kindness? or do you think there is never any honesty or benevolence in wise people? None of us, I hope, are so unhappy as to think that. Well, whatever bit of a wise man's work is honestly and benevolently done, that bit is his book, or his piece of art. It is mixed always with evil fragments—ill-done, redundant, affected work. But if you read rightly, you will easily discover the true bits, and those are the book. Now, books of this kind have been written in all ages by their greatest men,—by great readers, great statesmen, and great thinkers. These are all at your choice; and Life is short. You have heard as much before;—yet have you measured and mapped out this short life and its

436

A book is essentially not a talked thing, but a written thing; and written, not with a view of mere communication, but of permanence. The book of talk is printed only because its author cannot speak to thousands of people at once; if he could, he would—the volume is mere multiplication of his voice. You cannot talk to your friend in India; if you could, you would; you write instead: that is mere conveyance of voice. But a book is written, not to multiply the voice merely, not to carry it merely, but to perpetuate it. The author has something to say which he perceives to be true and useful, or helpfully beautiful. So far as he knows, no one has yet said it; so far as he knows, no one else can say it. He is bound to say it, clearly and melodiously if he may; clearly, at all events. In the sum of his life he finds this to be the thing, or group of things, manifest to him; —this, the piece of true knowledge, or sight, which his share of sunshine and earth has permitted him to seize. He would fain set it down for ever; engrave it on rock, if he could; saying, "This is the best of me; for the rest, I ate, and drank, and slept, loved, and hated, like another; my life was as the vapour, and is not; but this I saw and knew: this, if anything of mine, is worth your memory." That is his "writing"; it is, in his small human way, and with whatever degree of true inspiration is in him, his inscription, or scripture. That is a "Book." Perhaps you think no books were ever so written? But, again, I ask you, do you at all believe in honesty, or at all in kindness? or do you think there is never any honesty or benevolence in wise people? None of us, I hope, are so unhappy as to think that. Well, whatever bit of a wise man's work is honestly and benevolently done, that bit is his book, or his piece of art. It is mixed always with evil fragments—ill-done, redundant, affected work. But if you read rightly, you will easily discover the true bits, and those are the book. Now, books of this kind have been written in all ages by their greatest men,—by great readers, great statesmen, and great thinkers. These are all at your choice; and Life is short. You have heard as much before;—yet have you measured and mapped out this short life and its possibilities? Do you know, if you read this, that you cannot read that—that what you lose to-day you cannot gain to-morrow? Will you go and gossip with your housemaid, or your stable-boy, when you may talk with queens and kings; or flatter yourselves that it is with any worthy degree of consciousness of your own claims to respect, that you jostle with the hungry and common crowd for entrée here, and audience there, when all the while this eternal court is open to you, with its society, wide as the world, multitudinous as its days, the chosen, and the mighty, of every place and time? Into

544

ABCDEFGHIJKLMNOPQRSTUVWXYZÆŒ

ABCDEFGHIJKLMNOPQRSTUVWXYZ

ABCDEFGHIJKLMNOPQRSTUVX

ABCDEFGHIJKLMNOPQRSTU

ABCDEFGHIJKLMNOPQR

ABCDEFGHIJKLMNOP

ABCDEFGHIJKLMN

ABCDEFGHIJKL

ABCDEFGHI

ABCDEFG

ABCDE

M 2

126 Old Face Roman Capitals

127 Old Style Roman Capitals

ABCDEFGHIJKLMNOPQRSTUVWXYZ&

ABCDEFGHIJKLMNOPQRSTUVWX

ABCDEFGHIJKLMNOPQRSTU

ABCDEFGHIJKLMNOPQR

ABCDEFGHIJKLMNOP

ABCDEFGHIJKLMNO

ABCDEFGHIJKL

ABCDEFGHIJKL

ABCDEFGHIJ

ABCDEFG

ABCDEFGHIJKLMNOPQRSTUVWXYZÆ&

ABCDEFGHIJKLMNOPQRSTUVWXYZ

ABCDEFGHIJKLMNOPQRSTUVWXYZ

ABCDEFGHIJKLMNOPQRSTU

ABCDEFGHIJKLMNOPQRST

ABCDEFGHIJKLMNOP

ABCDEFGHIJKLMNOPQR

ABCDEFGHIJKLMNOP

ABCDEFGHIJKLMNOP

ABCDEFGHIJKLMN

ABCDEFGHIJKL

128 Modern Roman Capitals

129 Old French Roman Capitals

ABCDEFGHIJKLMNOPQRSTUVWXYZ

ABCDEFGHIJKLMNOPQRSTUV

ABCDEFGHIJKLMNOPQS

ABCDEFGHIJKLMN

ABCDEFGHIJK

ABCDEFGHI

ABCDEFG

ABCDE

ABC

ABCDEFGHIJKLMNOPQRSTUVWXYZ ABCDEFGHIJKLMNOPQRSTUVWXYZ

ABCDEFGHIJKLMNOPQRSTUVWXYZABCDEFGHIJKLMN

ABCDEFGHIKLMNOPQRSTUVWXYZABCDEF

ABCDEFGHIJKLMNOPQRSTUVWXYZ&

ABCDEFGHIJKLMNOPQRSW

ABCDEFGHIJKLM

ABCDEFGHIJKL

ABCDEFGI

ABCDEF

130 Flemish Roman Capitals

131 Old Face Italic

abcdefghijkklmnopqrſstuvvvwxyzææſßſhſkſtℰ abcdefghijkklmnopqrſstuvvw

AABBCCDDEEFGGHIƷKKLMMNNOPPꝬRRSTUVVWXYZÆ

abcdefghijkklmnopqrſstuvvvwwxyzææſßſhſkſtℰ abcdefghijkklmnopqrs

AABBCCDDEEFGGHIƷKKLMMNNOPPꝬRRSTTU

abcdefghijklmnopqrſstuvwxyzææſßſhſkſtℰ abcdefghijklmnopqrs

AABBCCDDEEFGGHIƷKKLMMNNOPPꝬRR

abcdefghijklmnopqrſstuvwxyzææſßſhſkſtℰ abcdefghijkl

AABBCCDDEEFGGHIƷKKLMMNNOPPꝬ

abcdefghijklmnopqrſstuvwxyzææſtſßſhſkſtℰ abcdefg

AABBCCDDEEFGGHIƷKKLMMNNO

abcdefghijklmnopqrſstuvwwxyzææſtſßſk

AABBCCDDEEFGGHIƷKKLM

abcdefghijklmnopqrſstuvwxyzææſt

AABBCCDDEEFGGHIƷK

abcdefghijkklmnopqrſstuvvww

AABBCCDDEEFGGHM

abcdefghijklmnopqrstuvwxyzææ&abcdefghijklmnopqrstuvwxyzææ&abcdefgh

ABCDEFGHIJKLMNOPQRSTUVWXYZÆŒABCDEFGHIJKLM

abcdefghijklmnopqrstuvwxyzææ&abcdefghijklmnopqrstuvwxyzææi

ABCDEFGHIJKLMNOPQRSTUVWXYZÆŒABCDEFGH

abcdefghijklmnopqrstuvwxyzææ&abcdefghijklmnopqrstuvwxyzæa

ABCDEFGHIJKLMNOPQRSTUVWXYZÆŒABCDE

abcdefghijklmnopqrstuvwxyzææ&abcdefghijklmnopqrstuvx

ABCDEFGHIJKLMNOPQRSTUVWXYZÆŒAI

abcdefghijklmnopqrstuvwxyzææ&abcdefghijklmnop

ABCDEFGHIJKLMNOPQRSTUVWXYZ

abcdefghijklmnopqrstuvwxyzææ&abcdefghi

ABCDEFGHIJKLMNOPQRSTUVWI

abcdefghijklmnopqrstuvwxyzææ&abc

ABCDEFGHIJKLMNOPQW

abcdefghijklmnopqrstuvwx

ABCDEFGHIJKLMNS

N

132 Old Style Italic

133 Modern Italic

abcdefghijklmnopqrstuvwxyzææabcdefghijklmnopqrstuvwxyzææabcdefi

ABCDEFGHIJKLMNOPQRSTUVWXYZÆŒABCDEFGHIJKL

abcdefghijklmnopqrstuvwxyzææabcdefghijklmnopqrstuvwxyzææabcdefi

ABCDEFGHIJKLMNOPQRSTUVWXYZÆŒABCDEFGHIJ

abcdefghijklmnopqrstuvwxyzææabcdefghijklmnopqrstuvwxyzææ&

ABCDEFGHIJKLMNOPQRSTUVWXYZÆŒABCDEFG

abcdefghijklmnopqrstuvwxyzææabcdefghijklmnopqrstuvwxyz

ABCDEFGHIJKLMNOPQRSTUVWXYZÆŒABCS

abcdefghijklmnopqrstuvwxyzææabcdefghijklmnopqrstu

ABCDEFGHIJKLMNOPQRSTUVWXYZÆA

abcdefghijklmnopqrstuvwxyzææabcdefghijklmnop

ABCDEFGHIJKLMNOPQRSTUVWXY

abcdefghijklmnopqrstuvwxyzææabcde

ABCDEFGHIJKLMNOPQRS

abcdefghijklmnopqrstuvwxyzæ

ABCDEFGHIJKLMNO

abcdefghijklmnopqrstuvwxyzabcdefghijklmnopqrstuvwxyzabcdefghijkn

ABCDEFGHJKLMNOPQRSTUVWXYZABCDEFGHJKL

abcdefghijklmnopqrstuvwxyzabcdefghijklmnopqrstw

ABCDEFGHJKLMNOPQRSTUVWXYZABJ

abcdefghijklmnopqrstuvwxyzabcdefghijklmno

ABCDEFGHJKLMNOPQRSTUVWXY

abcdefghijklmnopqrstuvwxyzctab

ABCDEFGHJKLMNOPQR

abcdefghijklmnopqrstuvwxyz

ABCDEFGHJKLMNI

abcdefghijklmnopqrstuv

ABCDEFGHJKLR

abcdefghijklmnopq

ABCDEFGHM

134 Old English Black Letter

135 Dutch Black Letter

abcdefghijklmnopqrsſtuvwxyzabcdefghijklmnopqrsſtuw

ABCDEFGHIJKLMNOPQRSCUVWXYZAB

abcdefghijklmnopqrsſtuvwxyz abcdefghijklmnopq

ABCDEFGHIJKLMNOPQRSCUVWXY

abcdefghijklmnopqrsſtuvwxyzabcdefghijkln

ABCDEFGHIJKLMNOPQRSCUX

abcdefghij klmnopqrsſtuvwxyzabcdef

ABCDEFGHIJKLMNOPQRS

abcdefghijklmnopqrsſtuvwxy

ABCDEFGHIJKLMNW

abcdefghijklmnopqrsſt

ABCDEFGHIKM

abcdefghijklmnopqr

ABCDEFGHIK

abcdefghijklmnopqrstuvwxyz3æœ&abcdefghijklm1234567890

ABCDEFGHIKLMNOPQRSTUVWXYZ ABCDEFGHI

abcdefghijklmnopqrstuvwxyz3æœ&abc1234567890

ABCDEFGHIKLMNOPQRSTUVWXYZ ABC

abcdefghijklmnopqrstuvwxyz3æœ&12345678

ABCDEFGHIKLMNOPQRSTUVWXY

abcdefghijklmnopqrstuvwxyz3&a

ABCDEFGHIKLMNOPQR

abcdeghijkmnopqrstuvwy

ABCDEFGHIKLMNW

abcdeghijklmnopqrw

ABCDEFGHIKN

abcdefghiklmnow

ABCDEFGHM

136 Tudor Black Letter

137 Venetian Text Black Letter

abcdefghijklmnopqrstuvwxyz§abcdefgi1234567890

ABCDEFGHIJKLMNOPQRSTUVWXYZABCDEFGHIW

abcdefghijklmnopqrstuvwxyz§abce1234567890

ABCDEFGHIJKLMNOPQRSTUVWXYZ ABCDEH

abcdefghijklmnopqrstuvwxyz 12

ABCDEFGHIJKLMNOPQRSTUV

abcdefghijklmnopqrstuv

ABCDEFGHIJKLMNOP

abcdefghijklmnopqr

ABCDEFGHIJKLMN

abcdefghijklnopu

ABCDEFGHIJKR

SAMPLES OF PAPERS

THE accompanying leaves of machine- and hand-made papers are given as specimens of papers of fair qualities, and they are here classed in their order of value—machine-made papers first, and those handmade in the second division—each kind being graded according to its value, which is based firstly on quality and secondly on weight. Papers being sold at so much per pound, the exact cost of a ream of paper is dependent on its size and gross weight. The paper on which this book is printed is ordinary antique laid 32 lb. demy. Machine papers can be made to any size, but the moulds for handmade papers only exist in certain dimensions.

Most of the papers shown here may be obtained from stock in several sizes. If they have to be made, colour and weight can be altered in most cases, and the length of time for making machine papers is usually one to two weeks—handmade papers possibly four to six weeks.

INDEX OF PAPER SAMPLES

Machine made

Handmade